Dad's Last Hunt

By

Sharon Larson (The Spouse)
&
Mike Larson (A Son)

Dementia – An Uninvited Guest
or
Alzheimer's – Not all It's Cracked Up to Be

ISBN-10: 0615563864
EAN-13: 9780615563862

Contents

The Last Hunt

Mike - October 20, 2005

Anticipation

Dad always wanted to shoot an elk. So this year Dad and I decided to join his hunting buddies on a trip to Wyoming in the middle of October. Part of what makes a trip fun is the anticipation and planning leading up to it. During the course of the summer we talked about the big elk we planned to shoot. Should we bring the ATV (all-terrain vehicle), which trailer, which truck, which guns (or do we need new guns), what ammo, which clothes? We discussed these questions again and again. By the time the trip came around, we had worked ourselves into a tizzy of anticipation.

Maybe even a little too excited. On Monday night, Dad told Mom that he didn't want to go. There were just too many things. Mom managed to talk him into going, but he was nervous. You see my Dad has exhibited irrational behavior for the last several years. His father had Alzheimer's and it tore Dad up seeing what it had done to him. Dad was greatly concerned he was going to suffer the same fate.

After several trips to the Mayo clinic and visits with a couple of other doctors, there was still no conclusive diagnosis. The best guess was that Dad had dementia in his frontal lobes. Classic Alzheimer's affects a person's temporal or side lobes, which destroys their memory, whereas the frontal lobes control behavior and decision making. That's where Dad has problems. So we don't think he has classic Alzheimer's, but some other kind of dementia.

1

Donny and Mike loading up for the Trip

Hit the Road

When Thursday finally rolled around, Dad and I loaded the truck with gear and set off for Wyoming. I didn't feel confident about Dad driving while we were pulling a trailer, so we split up the fifteen-hour drive into two days. Traveling together provided lots of opportunity to talk and talk we did.

We talked about the excitement of hiking in the mountains. I had been with Dad on approximately ten trips out west hunting for elk, mule deer, or antelope. Our typical hunt involved driving the truck or ATV as far as possible on a logging road before dawn, parking it, putting the keys on the tire in case not everyone makes it back, grabbing your gun and your pack and going for the day. Each person is self-sufficient and responsible for his own well-being. If you get hurt, you got problems, because you can't just call someone on a cell phone; there is no cell phone coverage.

There is something powerful, almost primal about hunting that way. Actually shooting an animal is a bonus. But the real thrill is hiking around with your gun and your pack.

My first trip out west was when I was fourteen; Dad gave me a five minute lesson on how to use a compass. Then he told me to meet him on the hill straight south of where we were standing. Somehow I managed to go to the right spot. That was the extent of my orienteering education. Dad told me to be back at the truck an hour before dark and we each went our separate ways. Dad always believed in throwing me into the deep end and letting me swim my way out.

During our drive, Dad said he felt like he could still out walk almost anybody. It was not like he was bragging or anything; he just had confidence he could do it. I didn't realize it at the time, but I think his condition gave him misplaced confidence, like that of a teenage boy who does not need to be told anything because he already knows it all.

On Friday we drove up into the Big Horn Mountains in bright sunlight and we could see for miles. The Big Horn Mountains are much older than the Rocky Mountains and thus are more weathered and the peaks more rounded. We stopped at a scenic overlook and marveled at how small the road looked so far below us.

We met up with our hunting group and scouted for a good place to hunt. We found a trail that went ten miles back into the boondocks. We drove the ATV back a couple miles and figured there would be prime elk habitat at the end of the trail.

Getting Organized

After scouting, we met back at the lodge. The lodge consisted of a main building with a bar and restaurant surrounded by a muddy parking lot and ten cabins. Lots of knotty pine and deer antler light fixtures. It was not "roughing it" by any means. The guests were predominantly men who were going hunting.

We unloaded our gear and figured out sleeping arrangements. We had all brought way more equipment than we would ever need. For example, one of the guys brought a mountain bike to get him into more remote locations where ATVs are not allowed. Theoretically this is a possibility, but in my experience, never a reality. Men like to complain that women over pack, but for a hunting trip, men are at least as guilty.

Dad and I shared a bedroom. As we got ourselves organized for the next day, Dad couldn't find his hunting license. But he did pull a pile of old shoelaces from his pocket. I asked him what in the world those were for and he said, "In case I need to tie anything up." I have seen men carry rope on hunts, but never old shoelaces.

Then he pulled a hunting knife from his other pocket, then another and another. It turned out that he brought four knives, all about the same. It reminded me of Christopher Robin stuffing his pockets with cool stuff before he went to visit Winnie the Pooh. You never know what might be useful on a big adventure...

During the course of the trip, Dad repeatedly misplaced his billfold, flashlight, medications, hunting license, ammo and other assorted items. It was a minor miracle we made it into the field with everything we were supposed to have.

Night Before the Hunt

Anyone who has been around a group of men before the opening of a big hunt has probably witnessed the magical transformation of men into boys. Our transformation happened when we went to the lodge to eat. We were just giddy with excitement. A hunter's best chance of getting an elk is the morning of the opener. After that, the elk get more wary. It can be hard to sleep the night before the season opener.

As we sat around the table getting reacquainted, all the problems of the outside world fell away. It was all good natured teasing and stories about past hunts. When the waitress came around to take our order, Dad made a square with his hands and pointed at the menu. The waitress looked quizzically at him, wondering if he was making a joke. I don't think he was joking. He wanted a hamburger but either he had difficulty articulating his order or was overwhelmed with camaraderie. I think the guys were starting to pick up on the fact that Dad was not his old self but nobody said anything.

There were lots of little things like that. Any one, taken individually, would not mean much. Taken together, they were evidence of the onset of his disease.

Let the Hunt Begin

On Saturday morning, we unloaded the ATV and started on our drive up the mountain. The road was in poor condition. It had snowed a couple of weeks earlier and the snow was partially melted, leaving it muddy with deep ruts. A four wheel drive pickup with chains could make it, but otherwise took an ATV. It was a rough ride for two men on an ATV designed for one. Because he didn't swear, Dad said, "Jyckus Patidilie! do you need to drive so fast on such a dumb road?"

When we got near the end of the trail, we stopped in an area that looked promising. It was an area that was burned out maybe five years ago and now the evergreens were about four feet high. Because I was concerned about Dad, I had convinced him that for the first morning, we would just "post" instead of hiking off alone. "Post" means that you sit in one place and wait till the elk walk by, instead of walking around trying to find them. Dad was posted at the bottom and I climbed to the top. At 9:00, we met back at the ATV. I showed Dad some tracks that looked fresh. Dad told me he had seen five elk, including a big bull. I asked, "Why didn't you shoot?" He said, "It just did not work out. They were about two hundred and fifty yards away, but it wasn't a clear shot." I told him he should shoot if he had the opportunity. I think he felt bad because he said, "Yeah, I guess I should've shot."

We decided to go for a drive on the ATV. When we were putting the guns into the case, I noticed that his safety was not on. When I questioned him, he claimed that he didn't use the safety on that gun. This was coming from the guy who taught gun training to hundreds of kids over the course of twenty years! It just didn't make sense. I knew that he knew better.

Later that afternoon I found an outcropping that overlooked an expansive valley full of pine trees and elk trails. I stretched out in the warm sun and had a glorious nap. There is something about sleeping in a deer stand that rejuvenates me. I did not see anything all day, but was happy that Dad had. I was even feeling a little proud of myself for finding the spot, even though I knew it was just luck.

Day 2 – The Hot Spot

When we got back to the cabin that night, we were the only ones who had seen any elk. We started making plans for more of our group to go to our area. We did our best to give the others good intelligence about our hot spot. We looked at topographical maps and planned who was going to post, who was going to drive, which direction to drive and at what time. You would have thought we were planning a military campaign the way we talked and strategized.

The next morning Dad and I went to our hot spot early per the plan. About ten minutes after getting settled Dad shot. About five minutes later he shot again. I thought that was a good sign. What we say in Minnesota is that one shot is usually a kill. Typically, when you hear many shots together, it's a miss. A second shot five minutes after the first was normally used to finish off the animal.

But Dad wasn't done shooting yet. While he was shooting, I saw two animals across the meadow. I thought it odd that they did not take off running when he was shooting. I looked at them through my scope, then through the binoculars and was pretty sure they were moose. Moose are not the smartest creatures in the woods and we did not have a license to hunt them. It never occurred to me that Dad was shooting at them.

About this time the rest of our group showed up and I heard one of them say, "Donny, those are moose." Dad had fired five rounds at the moose and, thankfully, did not hit them. He told one of the guys, "I usually don't take so many shots to hit something."

The other guys in our group went over and verified there was no blood.

I was worried that Dad would be embarrassed about having shot at the wrong kind of animal. But his comment to me when we got back together was, "I'm glad I shot." I don't think he was glad he shot because of some macho thing, but because I had scolded him the day before. It seemed like he was trying to do something to make me happy.

Dad confirmed that the five "elk" he had seen the previous day were in fact moose. That admission severely depleted the group's optimism. It meant no one had seen an elk so far and not much for fresh sign.

Salt of the Earth

Dad has been hunting with this group of guys for the last thirty years. They are "salt of the earth" kind of guys. They like to give one another a hard time about any and everything. For example, one time I was told to bring blaze orange toilet paper; otherwise, another hunter might mistake me for a white tail deer.

As far as I know, the group did not react to Dad shooting at the wrong animal. They did not get mad, or give him a hard time, both of which probably would have occurred if it had been someone else. I am sure that by this point in the trip, they all realized Dad was not thinking completely rationally.

After lunch we went for a ride in the pickups up a different side of the mountain. I drove by myself on the ATV and, it turns out, that was one of the more enjoyable aspects of the trip, at least for me. Dad and I split from the group and went back to our spot. It may not have been the "hot spot," but we figured it was as good a place as any.

The Big Walk

We arrived back at our spot at 1:30 and it didn't get dark until 6:30, so we decided not to post right away. Dad is notorious for not liking to sit still for more than an hour and I knew he loved to walk.

We parked the ATV and walked north. After half an hour, we crossed a creek and entered a broad meadow. Dad said we should split and meet at the top of the next mountain but I said that we should keep together. We hiked through some beautiful country and ran into two hunters on horseback. They looked like they could have been on the cover of a hunting magazine. Their gear, their packs, their horses, their guns in their gun holsters, everything was perfect. They reminded me of the guy with the Guci saddlebags in the movie Blazing Saddles. They asked how we got there because we were pretty far off the beaten track.

Then we started to go up another mountain where there was an opening about 1,200 yards long and 300 yards wide. Dad walked up one side with me on the other. We saw a coyote and enjoyed the scenery. We met up at the top as planned, but Dad was sweating profusely and said we better head back. We sat down to rest and drank some water from our water bottles.

I pride myself on being an expert with my GPS. I don't know how much expertise is really required to walk back to a waypoint, but I like to think I can do it as well as anybody. The use of a GPS, however, was not really required. The sun was shining bright and there was a road running to our south. I cheated and looked at the GPS just to make sure.

We walked slowly and had a couple more water breaks. We came to an outcropping that looked like a big butt because it had a crack down the middle. We laughed about it and kept going. Dad, for the most part, was following me, but he was on the left. We could hear the ATVs on the road so I knew we were not far away.

Somehow Dad veered farther left and I lost sight of him. I started going to the left to find him but I couldn't see him. I thought that maybe he knew what he was doing so I found my way back to the ATV but he was not there. I drove the ATV up and down the road thinking maybe he would hear it and walk toward it.

It was now 3:30 and I started thinking about what could happen. Dad had on just a thin coat because we did not want to get overheated when walking. But what concerned me more was that he might not be thinking rationally. He might get frustrated and start walking through the thick woods and just keep going because he was mad.

I decided to try to find him. I made a loop to where I thought he would most likely be, but did not find him. I went back to the ATV and drove up and down the road a couple more times. Finally, at 4:30 I decided to take more drastic action. I figured it would take an hour for help to arrive and that would only give us an hour until dark. So I fired three shots into the air, which is the hunter's distress signal, but did not hear any shots in response. The response I was waiting for was one shot to indicate that my shots were heard.

I then flagged down a man and his son in a big four-wheel drive truck and told them I needed help because my dad was lost. This man really turned out to be a Good Samaritan. He said he would go and get the United States Forest Service.

Promises Made

I anticipated the worst. I fully expected that Dad would die out there that night. I kind of pushed him into going on the trip and now it would result in tragedy. What will my family say? What more should I have done to prevent this from happening?

I could imagine people saying, "What was Mike thinking? He brought his Dad, who is not all there, out into the woods, left him with minimal clothing, no food and little water. I'm not surprised Mike screwed up, but I didn't think his poor judgment would cost his Dad his life."

I prayed more than a few prayers and made some promises that if he could just get out of this, I'd try to do better.

Knowing help was on the way, I went back into the woods. I found the big butt rock and started trying to follow his footsteps in the snow. There was not enough snow to follow them but it got me started in the right direction. Every so often I would yell out "Dad!" hoping he would hear me.

I came to one of the broad meadows on the side of the mountain and something in my head told me to go around the next corner. I did and there was Dad walking up the hill. "I think I got a little lost," he said. He was soaking wet and cold. I gave him my coat and walked back in just a tee shirt.

As we walked back to the ATV, it occurred to me that this would be the last hunt like this my Dad should go on. He was not capable of taking care of himself in the woods and he would never want to be led around like a kid. My tears flowed freely, but I was careful not to let him see. When we got to the ATV I went into the woods where we had stashed the heavy coats and tried to collect myself. I made him take off all his shirts and gave him a dry fleece jacket and a heavy hunting coat. He seemed to warm up quickly and was in good spirits.

Back Into the World

We started down the mountain on the ATV and met the Good Samaritan who was bringing back help. He said, "It took me an hour, but I got the U. S. Forest Service for you." I explained that I had found Dad and thanked him for all he had done. His name was Thomas Pointon of Riverton Wyoming and I owe him a debt of gratitude.

Then I talked to the Forest Service woman. She had a big dog that I assume was a search specialist. I explained that I had found Dad and that everything was okay. She gave my Dad a good long look and told me to keep an eye on him. Then she told Dad to take care of himself and left.

All during these discussions Dad showed zero embarrassment about being lost. In fact he was kind of friendly to everyone. I think if this had happened to him before the onset of his disease he would have been embarrassed.

Later I found out that Dad did hear me fire the three shots into the air. Then he fired a shot back, but shot it into the ground so he did not goof up the hunting for anybody. I think if Dad called 911 he might say, "Sorry to bother you, but if you are not too busy, stop over at my house because it's on fire."

That night our group gathered around the table in our cabin and I recounted the story. I am not sure if it was a factor, but we decided to cut the trip short and go home. It had snowed two weeks prior to our arrival and all the elk had gone to their winter feeding grounds where we could not hunt. In any case, I was ready to go home.

When we parted ways with our group, several of them told me something to the effect that they were proud of me for taking care of my Dad the way that I did. I thanked them and told them it had been a great trip.

When we got home, I told Mom the story. After I left, she asked Dad if he was glad he went and he said, "The hunting was a lot of work, but I sure had a good time with Mike."

Next year we'll plan a fishing trip.

Hunting Buddies ready to go Home

Spouse, Nurse, Caregiver

Sharon

As a Registered Nurse and the Director of Nurses at our local hospital, I had a front row seat for thirty-four years to the drama that is played out in hospitals. Babies are born, some people get better and some people die. As a nursing professional, you feel better equipped than other people to deal with your family's health. As it turned out, in some ways, being a nurse just made what I was to experience more difficult.

I decided early in my husband Donny's disease to document behaviors and drugs so that when we went to see a doctor, I could provide relatively detailed information to assist the doctor. Those observations make up a lot of what I have written in this book.

I am also Donny's wife and as time went on, I became his primary caregiver. The entire concept of "till death do us part" has special significance to me based on my experience. The first chapter of this book took place in 2005. His mental decline started before that.

The Dawn of the New Reality

Sharon – November 2000

Donny had experienced pain in his knees for a long time. He'd injured one knee playing football in high school and the other knee playing softball in the "old men's league." I knew that if he had a "bone on bone" problem in his knees, it was very painful and he needed bilateral replacement of his knees. He opted to have both knees done at the same time so he wouldn't need to have a second surgery. The operation was scheduled the day before Thanksgiving. It was uneventful, but overnight Donny became confused and combative. The hospital staff attributed this behavior to the morphine. I was told it was not an allergic reaction, but he had intolerance to morphine.

After the operation, he was experiencing a lot of surgical pain. He was angry and told me he just wanted to die. The doctors tried different pain medications. Some of them made him as confused and incoherent as he had been on morphine. Since I was frustrated with his care, I wanted to blame somebody for screwing up the surgery. I also felt helpless, watching my husband in pain, confused and incoherent.

I had seen how visitors often boosted the spirits of patients. That was not the case in our situation. I ran into some friends in the hospital waiting room and told them that Donny wasn't ready for visitors. He would have only lashed out at them.

Thanksgiving

Three of my kids came home for the Thanksgiving holiday. They visited their Dad in the hospital and he was ornery. We tried our best to cheer him up. My sons told him he would be able walk without pain as long as he got a lube job for his new knees every six months. He didn't laugh, but they got a smile out of him. I cried many times during the Thanksgiving holiday. The operation that was supposed to make him better was turning into a nightmare.

The week after Thanksgiving, the doctors said I could take him home. He was still not able to walk on his own and his spirits had not improved much. Our old farm house was never designed for a wheelchair so just getting him into the house was a challenge. I had neighbors, a father and a son, carry Donny up the stairs and into the house. I'd set up a hide-a-bed on the main floor. Because the bathroom was upstairs, I'd rented a commode to make his care more convenient.

His first night home, however, the weirdness started. He got up in the middle of the night and managed to walk outside. Once there, he urinated off the front steps. It was about minus thirty degrees outside. Because I heard the front door open, I was able to get him back to bed.

The next morning I decided that there was something wrong with his medications and how they were affecting his mental status. I called on the neighbors again and they carried him to my car. I took him back to the emergency room, but they wouldn't keep him in the hospital. They advised that we have him evaluated for other mental or physical problems and suggested that he see several specialists including a neurologist, an internal medicine doctor, a urologist and also to continue seeing the orthopedic surgeon.

Thank God for caring neighbors; once again I had to call them. Then I took care of Donny at home for the next several weeks without any more big problems. It seemed like the morphine and other pain medications had lingered in his system. It was three weeks before he became oriented to place and time. A CT of his head showed that he'd had several small strokes, age undetermined. Maybe they happened as a result of the surgery; maybe they'd occurred years earlier. All I wanted was to get my Donny back, the way he was before.

Multiple Generations of Dementia

Mike

Dad is the fourth generation Larson to live in Pope County. Generation one, Gustav, homesteaded a farm in the 1870s. Their first winter, they lived in a sod hut dug into the side of a hill. It's a beautiful location on Lake Swenoda, named because it was surrounded by Swedes, Norwegians and Danes.

Generation two, Martin, died young. Generation three, David, had to quit school after the eighth grade to run the farm. Somehow David managed to purchase the adjoining farm, so he must have had some success as a farmer.

After Grandpa David's funeral, a guy came up to me and said that he knew my Grandpa when he was young. There was going to be a fight in the pool hall but Grandpa diffused the situation. He said that was the kind of guy my Grandpa was.

Another story I heard about my Grandpa is that he and his friends were "the men about town." They would dress up in fancy clothes including spats which covered the upper shoe and ankle and fastened underneath with a strap. Once ready, they would drive to town in their freshly washed car and do what they did back in the 1940's. I am not sure what they did in town, but I would guess it was similar to what I did when I went to town in the 1980's.

I don't know the story about how my Grandpa and Grandma met. But I do know that Grandma was two months pregnant when they got married and that he was seven years older than she was. I'm sure it must have been a scandal.

I have the impression that Grandpa David did not settle down right away. He told stories about how he and other local farmers

17

had boxing and wrestling matches in Sedan, a nearby small village. He said he was the top guy at his weight class.

When Dad was seven, Grandpa David quit drinking. Grandma said he'd quit for his kids' benefit. The only thing he had to drink the rest of his life was wine at communion. When I was growing up, Dad wouldn't drink in front of Grandpa. I was impressed that Dad respected Grandpa enough to change his behavior.

Grandpa lived through the depression and it influenced him the rest of his life. He was always tight with his money and was convinced that "hard times are coming again." I am sure my Dad heard that many times growing up.

My siblings and I spent a lot of time at Grandma and Grandpa's house. I hunted deer there in the fall, rode snowmobiles there in the winter and walked there in the summer. All year round we played cards together and ate. Always we ate.

Grandma had donuts or cookies or something sweet. Grandma was famous for two things: her donuts and her buns. It was a recurring joke to ask Grandma about her buns. "Grandma has the best buns around." "Are Grandma's buns hot?"

The other thing she was famous for was her donuts. She made them from scratch and they were better than anything at a bakery. Until the time she mistakenly used soap instead of flour. Then we teased her saying that her donuts made us talk with bubbles.

In 1974, when I was twelve years old, Grandpa and Grandma sold their farm. Grandpa bought Grandma an electric organ and a year later, a prefabricated house. I guess that was Grandma's reward for all her years of work.

Their house always reverberated with happy vibes. Whenever we stopped by, Grandma and Grandpa were always nice to one another and were always glad to see us. I don't ever remember a mean word being said in their house.

My other grandparents lived in a much different house. Grandpa Joe had a loud voice and was always mad about something. I remember hearing him as he drove the tractor in the field a half-mile in front of our house. He always talked to himself and was usually disgusted about something.

Grandpa David liked to smoke a pipe. When he drove the car, he'd have to light his pipe before driving. He often forgot to put the fire out and would put a still lit pipe into his shirt pocket. Most of his shirts had a burn-hole in the pocket. I don't know if that was an early sign of Alzheimer's or just a relatively harmless incident that brought Grandma consternation and the rest of us some laughs.

Déjà vu all Over Again

When I was first married and brought Karen over to visit them, the conversation went something like this:

Grandpa asked Karen, "What does your Dad do?" Karen said her Dad worked at the *Star Tribune*. Grandpa said that he remembered when a subscription to the newspaper cost $0.25. He then asked how much it cost now and we'd answer. Then he'd say in his Norwegian accent "Uff-da, dat's a lot ya know."

That exact conversation, with maybe just a couple of different words, repeated itself at least seven times. Toward the end of his life, we'd repeat the conversation a couple of times per visit. My impression is that people with Alzheimer's tend to ask the same questions over and over again and since the responses tend to be the same, the exact same conversation happens over and over again.

I sometimes teased Grandpa. For example, I told him he looked like the Pillsbury dough boy on the commercials because he had a little paunch. However, he never got riled. He'd always smile or make a joke. He was as easy going as could be. He couldn't remember things, but he laughed and then the problem went away.

I think we knew something was wrong with Grandpa. However, the word "Alzheimer's" was never spoken, at least as far as I know. In fact, I was kind of oblivious to what was going on. I was living several hours away and busy in my own life. So when I was told that Grandpa was put into the retirement home because he had Alzheimer's, I was surprised. Not so much that he had Alzheimer's, but that he had to go to the retirement home. They said he uri-nated in the closet and that Grandma couldn't handle it anymore.

In hindsight, I think that Grandma had been providing care for Grandpa for years and that none of us knew the toll it was tak-ing on her and her health. Grandpa was always easy to get along with and seemed so normal, that no one ever thought it was a problem for Grandma.

The community at large was probably even more shocked. They saw Grandpa in church and he was still driving and they probably thought he was in good shape. So when Grandpa was moved to the Rainbow room (Alzheimer's wing) at the nursing home, it was no doubt a surprise.

Over the next several years, Grandpa had some minor health problems. One time, he had an operation which required a hospi-tal stay. The day after surgery, Mom asked him how he was doing after the surgery and Grandpa said, "What surgery?" He had no recollection of the surgery that had happened just a day before. His body was healthy for a man his age and his lack of memory helped him recover quickly.

Dad did not deal well with Grandpa being in a nursing home. He rarely went to visit. Dad said he wanted to remember his Dad the way he was, not the way he was now.

Grandpa was in the nursing home for eight years. The longer he was there, the less I went to visit him. I don't even remember the last time I saw him. When he died in 1997, it was almost a re-lief. It seemed like he had been gone a long time before he died. I said a eulogy at his funeral. The main point was that he had lived a good life before the disease took his mind away from him. Grandma was at the funeral and she seemed sad but happy that he was in a better place.

The Old Folks Home

Glenwood Retirement Village (GRV)

Mike

As the name implies, the GRV is located in Glenwood, a town of 2,500 in west central Minnesota. Many people who live in Glenwood believe Garrison Keillor was using "Lake Wobegon" as a pseudonym for "Glenwood." Glenwood has two retirement homes: GRV and Lakeview Care Center. Historically GRV was for Lutherans, the Lakeview Home for Catholics.

Garrison does a great job of describing the differences between Lutherans and Catholics in a small town. In my experience, the biggest difference was food. My girlfriend's Catholic church had a pig roast with a keg of beer on a Saturday afternoon. My Lutheran church had potluck dinners after church with twelve different kinds of hot dishes that contained either cream of mushroom or tomato soup.

Both retirement homes have beautiful views of Lake Minnewaska. (Catholics have a little better view). Both are circled by bike trails which go through a park, over near the lake and back again.

Another author, Eleanor Cooney described her visit to a retirement home in California as "night of the living dead on promenade." I know exactly what she is talking about. The Glenwood homes have a certain amount of that, as I assume all must, but overall, I think both are very good retirement homes.

Being Lutheran, our family gravitated toward the GRV. GRV has all the amenities you would look for in a retirement home including a chapel, multiple pianos, a swing for people in wheel chairs, a big bird cage and a spacious lounge area. It even has a pontoon boat on which to give residents rides during the summer. It also has a separate wing for people with Alzheimer's disease called the Rainbow Room. The primary differences between the Rainbow room and the regular retirement wings are that the Rainbow Room is quieter and is locked so residents can't wander out.

The GRV has housed a number of us Larsons over the years as well as well as several of my Mom's family.

Grandma Larson

Mike

Grandpa David, was moved to the Rainbow Room of the GRV with Alzheimer's in 1989. Grandma recovered from the stress of being the primary caregiver and enjoyed ten years of independent living on the farm. She was always a good worker. In her day, I think Grandma could outwork most men. She would drive tractor, haul bales, gather eggs and butcher chickens. Dad said that when they shot pheasants, they would just give them to Grandma to clean. She cleaned the chickens so why not the pheasants. I have suggested this to my wife but she has a different attitude about cleaning my pheasants.

Before Grandpa left the farm, he had bought a brand new Mercury Marquis. Grandma loved that car. It was big and had a smooth ride. She drove all over the place. She lived by herself on the farm until 1999 when her kids decided she should not stay there. Against Grandma's wishes, they moved her to a low rent high-rise in Glenwood.

Grandma warmed up to the new location after she got there. There were always lots of old ladies and a few old men ready to play cards. She knew many of the people and seemed to have a good time. Each morning the residents put a sign on the outside door saying, "I'm okay." She went to the senior citizens center almost every day for lunch and made herself a meal at night. She kept her car in the attached parking lot and continued to drive her friends around. Grandma told me she preferred driving because some of the other old ladies couldn't drive so well.

Finally the Mercury broke down. It was going to be expensive to get it fixed and her kids convinced her that they should just sell it. Grandma was encouraged to ride the senior citizen's bus. She missed her car but didn't complain. Grandma complained less than anyone I know.

Grandma lived in the high-rise for five years. Then she started having problems taking her medications correctly, had numerous bladder infections and was not as sharp mentally as she had been. In 2004 it was decided she needed to move to an assisted living facility where meals were provided. They also monitored her medicine. This lasted for about two years. In 2006, she fell several times during the night and there wasn't enough night staff to keep her safe. The staff recommended that she be moved to the GRV, and so she was moved.

Grandma in the GRV

Grandma was never diagnosed with any form of dementia. However, her mind seemed to go in and out of reality. She said that she knew Grandpa was in another part of the building and had taken up with another woman. Later, she identified another male resident as being David, but said he was ignoring her. She even approached him one day and asked if he didn't recognize her. Of course he didn't and this made her mad–and sad. When that resident died, so did her fantasy of him being David. She never talked about him again.

Grandma often talked about her Mom as if she were alive and said that she had talked to her. She had very vivid, disturbing dreams and couldn't accept that they were just dreams. Eventually, she'd ask if her Mom had died because she couldn't remember her funeral. When told that her mom and David had both died, she'd say, "Everybody has left me." But she always recognized everyone in the family and was always glad to see us. She might ask, "Who is your wife again?" I think she knew me and knew that I was married, just couldn't place the names.

For some reason Grandma liked to sit in a chair in the main intersection of the retirement home. I think she liked the activity, all the comings and goings. She told me about the staff romances. I don't know if she only imagined the romances, but if half of what Grandma told me was true, there was a lot of drama at the GRV.

At some point, Grandma became more agitated by all the activity. Her case worker recommended that we move Grandma to the Rainbow Room because it was quieter and Grandma would be less stimulated. So Grandma made the move to where her husband had been several years earlier.

As Grandma aged, she progressed from one living arrangement to the next, each time getting more services and less independence. I think she would have preferred to stay at each stage longer then she did. She was never ready to move to the next stage but the world kind of moved her along despite her wishes.

Best Mother-in-Law

Sharon

Donny's mom, Sylvia to me, was a wonderful person. I often told people that she was the best mother-in-law a person could have. My own mother was killed in a car accident when I was thirty-four. At the time, we had four young children. It was a great shock and a terrible time for me. Grandma Sylvia filled a big void. She became like a mother to me and became very close to my children. She and David lived only two miles from us and we visited one another frequently.

Donny was exceptionally close to both his parents, especially his mother. She always catered to his every need and was very protective of him all of his life. She and David helped him with the bees when he needed help. They would have done anything for him.

As his parents got older, Donny made an effort to get there every single day, usually in time for tea and cookies or doughnuts. He teased her that if her cookie jar was empty, he wouldn't come back until she had more sweets on hand. By that afternoon, she'd call and tell him she was ready for him again and Donny would just smile.

Dad's Destiny

Mike

We would go to visit Grandma at the GRV. On one visit there, a lady was playing the piano. We were there for an hour and she never played the same song twice. She played classical music like a professional. When we were getting ready to leave, one of the nurse's aides went over and asked her if she was ready for her snack. She was a resident.

On another visit a lady came and sat very close to me, closer than was comfortable. I'm not sure what she said, but my impression was that she wanted me to go to her room for sex. These people are the ultimate in vulnerability. They wouldn't even remember being abused.

In general people in a nursing home seemed starved for conversation. Whenever I visited someone, a couple of other residents wheeled themselves over to the table to talk. They loved to talk. They were also very good listeners. I always tried to tell them about the weather, the fishing, the hunting, pretty much anything. It's the only place I've been where even I am a brilliant conversationalist.

Grandma told me that she now had her meals at the same table as Art Dickson. Art used to live near Grandma and went to her church. So they were friends and she wanted to stay at the same table with him. Art pushed her around in her wheelchair and thought it was his job to watch out for her. They ate together until Art started eating her food. Then the staff had to separate them. Evidently who you sat with at meal time was important. I guess we always are cognizant of our social standing and we want to be in the right group.

Not that the residents were always nice. One time a male resident kicked at my Mom and another one punched her in the arm to get her attention. Several times, residents tried to sneak out. The security code to unlock the door was 5-7-8-6-*. Sometimes residents would sit there hoping a visitor wouldn't notice they were there and could escape.

Dad would visit Grandma at the GRV every once in a while, probably more often than he visited his Dad at the GRV. During the visits when I was there, Dad was always quiet. I think that at some level he knew the GRV was his destiny.

When Did It Start?

Mike

Like a lot of men, Dad had a selective memory. He'd ask Mom, "Where is the ketchup?" or "Are we doing anything this weekend?" Mom would say the ketchup was in the door, right in front of him and they were going to Braatens on Saturday night. I don't think that was Alzheimer's, but more like lazy thinking or prioritizing what was important.

Dad got into the beekeeping business because his best friend was in the business. The business did okay over the years and Dad was a good provider for his family. Although Dad always said it worked because Mom had a stable job as Director of Nurses at the hospital.

Dad graduated from high school but did not go to college. However, he felt strongly that his kids should go to school. Unlike Elton John's Dad in "Goodbye Yellow Brick Road," mine did not want me to stay down on the farm.

Mom and I have had conversations trying to pinpoint when we first noticed unusual behavior. He made some poor business decisions, like putting another axel on a truck that ended up costing money without providing any benefit, but everybody in business makes poor business decisions from time to time.

I remember him getting frustrated easily. And I remember him being very sensitive to ridicule. For example, he was grilling hamburgers at the hospital barbeque and one of his friends made a comment about Dad's technique. Dad played along with the joke, but I could tell he didn't like it.

Dad always kept things to himself. He was part of the generation where men didn't share their feelings. Before 2003, Dad never expressed concern to Mom or anyone else that he was worried about losing his mind to Alzheimer's or Dementia.

Dad sold his beekeeping business in 1994. The original buyer was able to complete only half of the transaction. There was a good honey crop the next year and Dad was able to sell the balance to a second buyer for a little bit more money than he would have received from the first buyer. I think Dad did a good job of negotiating with the two buyers and avoiding a lawsuit. Later on, however, Dad came to believe he had been cheated out of something. It became one of Dad's familiar rants: "I don't think I got everything I was supposed to!"

Over the next couple of years, Dad started buying things. One time at an auction sale, he bought a big disc that was way too big to be pulled behind his tractor. But he bought mostly smaller items like his infamous grease guns. He had eight of them. I don't know if any worked, but he always said they could be fixed.

After a while Mom asked Norman to stop bringing Dad to the Belgrade flea market on Tuesday mornings. My uncle said it best when he said that Donny had become very acquisitive.

I am not sure if any of the above are symptoms of the disease or if they were just normal behavior. In fact I can't point to one thing and say that is when the disease started. But I don't think it hit all at once. My sense is that it slips into a person's behavior a little bit at a time. In Dad's case, over a period of many years.

Sell the Farm

Mike

It's a tradition in our neck of the woods that after you retire, you sell the farm and move to town. My Mom was tired of living twelve miles from town and wanted to retire closer to town. Dad felt equally as strongly that they should stay on the farm. It seemed like he planned to fill up his three big pole barns with treasure and then spend his twilight years wandering around organizing and sorting.

Thus began a family crisis. My siblings and I tried to be supportive to both our parents and not take sides. We looked for a compromise by suggesting that maybe they could remodel the farm house. However, there was no bathroom on the main floor and Dad's bad knees made the stairs a challenge for him to climb, so that argument was shot down.

At that time, we didn't yet have a diagnosis of dementia for Dad. However, we were all aware that something was not right with him. Selling the farm would take away his security and everything he held dear. We were concerned that moving would only accelerate his downward spiral.

We never had an official family meeting, but the decision was made to have an auction sale and sell the farm. We told Dad that he had chosen where they lived for the first thirty years and Mom got to choose for the next thirty years. Also, Mom told him that wherever they moved would have at least one out-building, so Dad could have a shop.

The auction sale was traumatic for our family. It was scheduled for a Saturday in the spring. For several days before the sale, we

29

organized, sorted and cleaned all kinds of different things (including the grease guns). We even found some time to race Dad's old pickup truck around the pole barn in the dirt. We figured it was no use to play it safe at this point.

In a farm auction, your neighbors assign a dollar value to many of your worldly possessions. The farmer usually makes himself scarce on that day and that was definitely the case for Dad. He was not in favor of the auction to begin with. I'm sure he felt like his family was selling him out, literally.

Dad Warmed to the Idea

Sharon

It took several years to sell our farm and during that time we looked at many, many houses and even thought about building a new one. Nothing seemed to be just right, but we weren't in a position to do anything until we sold our farm. We were in Texas when we got the call that there was an offer on our farm, which was very exciting. We packed our things and headed home to find a place to live. Our realtor told us about a new listing she thought would be perfect for us. We both fell in love with it at first sight and that was the end of our searching. We moved there in June 2003.

It was my dream house. Donny was happy with the outside buildings where he could have a wood working shop and lots of storage room. He also started planning how and where he would plant trees, a passion of his. He planted, watered and weeded 1,000 trees by hand. People still talk to me about how nice Donny's trees look and how they remember him out there working.

Just Tell Me What's Wrong

Sharon – December 2003

Specialists

I had a bad visit with a neurologist that still upsets me when I think about it. He asked me if Donny was able to balance the checkbook. All of our married life I had managed our checkbook because Donny didn't want to do it. He worked hard outside and thought I could write the checks and do the bookwork. He'd grown up in a home where his mother did the bookwork for the same reasons I was doing it. The neurologist lit into me implying that I was the cause of his problems. I was enabling him because I didn't allow him that responsibility.

Each specialist evaluated Donny in his own area of expertise and nothing definitive showed up. It seemed to me there was no collaboration at all between them. One doctor told me he couldn't prescribe any pain medicine for him, but that I should instead talk to the internal medicine doctor. This back and forth between specialists was frustrating and it was a great relief to go back to our family practice doctor who reviewed all the reports. He'd been caring for Donny for many years which made it easier to see the whole picture. He knew what medications had worked in the past and what medications had given him problems.

Alzheimer's?

I talked to our family practice doctor about the possibility of Donny having Alzheimer's. I said that he was having mood swings and short-term memory loss. He'd also lost interest in many things and was unable to do tasks that he'd done many times before The doctor told us that symptoms of depression were similar to Alzheimer's and started him on Zoloft. By December of 2003, he was sleeping excessively and still had bad mood swings. The doctor switched him over to Prozac. That didn't help at all.

We went to Texas for the winter, which is what he wanted to do. Things went all right for a while, but he lost interest in golfing and other activities and continued to sleep excessively. We've played bridge for many years and he's always been good at it. We played several times down there. One night it would be fine and another night it was really bad. On the bad nights, it was like he had never played the game before. Again, he had severe mood swings. All he wanted to do was to go home, so we left earlier than we'd planned.

On the way home, Donny had a really bad spell. It was the second day out and we thought we heard a strange noise in the car. We pulled into a service station, but the mechanic couldn't find anything wrong with our car. I took the keys for the car and Donny panicked because he didn't know how to get home from where we were.

"I asked the mechanic how to get to Morris and he doesn't know where Morris is," Donny said. Morris is a town thirty miles from our home in Minnesota, which was still a couple of states away. We had never traveled through Morris before, either coming or going to Texas. I was really scared, but I assured him that I knew where to go.

We went back and forth for a good fifteen minutes as I tried to calm him down. I finally said, "Please trust me," and he woefully replied, "Will you take me to my home?" At that moment, I don't think he really knew who I was. I told him he was very confused and needed to rest a while. Road signs confused him too, but when he saw the sign "Welcome to Minnesota", he finally relaxed and slept the rest of the way home. Once there, he was much better, happy to be home and in familiar surroundings.

During the ride home, I heard a discussion about a study which showed a relationship between taking Prozac and suicide. Man, did that give me something to think about. The first thing I did when I got home was make a doctor's appointment for him. After the doctor's interview with us, he said he was fairly certain that Donny had Alzheimer's. Don's response was, "I told you so." His dad had it and he always felt that he would have it too. He was taken off the Prozac at that time. A CT of his head was done and there was no change since the last CT.

On April 20th, Donny was started on Aricept. In two weeks I noticed an improvement. His mood swings were not as severe and even laughed and joked occasionally, which I hadn't heard for a long time.

Tentative Diagnosis

Sharon – May 2004

After much persuasion from my children, we went to Rochester to see if there was anything to be done for Donny. After several days of tests, we met with the lead doctor who is a neurologist that specializes in memory disorders. He said he would send a detailed report to Don's primary physician.

The MRI showed several additional small strokes since the MRI done in December 2000. It also showed that there was some atrophy in the frontal lobes. He said that small strokes are fairly common in older people and they often are the start of some type of dementia.

The doctor felt that Donny had frontal lobe dementia, or Pick's Disease. Frontal lobe dementia affects the behavior and Alzheimer's affects the memory. He says Pick's Disease progresses slower than Alzheimer's and in his opinion, was not hereditary. It was of prime importance to keep his blood pressure and his cholesterol within acceptable limits. He said the medications he was on were the right ones, but to increase the Vitamin E to 1000 mg bid. He felt there was still some depression and recommended Lexapro to treat symptoms.

There was a new med on the market called Nemanda, which he wouldn't recommend at this point. He was pleased that Donny was on Aricept.

Donny felt very relieved that he didn't have Alzheimer's and the doctor didn't really get into telling us about Pick's disease. He told me several times to read about it on the internet. I think he didn't want Donny to know any more than what he told us. I was feeling pretty good about the news until I read more about it. It's not a pretty picture.

He had a pacemaker put in on August 3, 2005 and that kept him inactive for a couple of weeks. He had complications of cellulitis from his IV line, then atelectasis in his lower left lung and after he was done with the antibiotics for his cellulitis, he developed pneumonia. After these problems were all resolved, I was pleased that the pacemaker still worked fine.

Subtle Changes Over Time

Sharon – August 2005

Since Don's visit to the Mayo Clinic in May of 2004, there have been subtle changes in his behavior. His short-term memory is not great, but that's not a huge problem. The main problems were his great mood swings and his need to sleep excessively. The two were related as when he was depressed, he could sleep up to 12-16 hours a night. Our family doctor started him on Provigil, a medication used to treat narcolepsy or excessive sleeping.

Other symptoms persisted and had gotten progressively worse. He'd lost interest in many activities that he used to enjoy. He didn't want to play golf, cards, or go out to eat. He was withdrawing from our social contacts. It became very difficult for him to express himself and, consequently, he remained very quiet, especially in a group. We were with a group of our friends last week and he made the comment, "You know I'm not able to visit with them anymore. It's like I can't keep up with them."

He used to be a great "handy man", but now he can't figure out simple repair jobs. For example, repairing the lawn mower, the vacuum cleaner, or an automobile were things he used to be able to do which now frustrated him. Another example would be that he was not able to start the lawn mower by himself all spring despite the fact that I'd shown him ten to fifteen times. Another day I found him in the pickup trying to start it and he didn't have his key in the starter.

He obsessed about different things. He was sure something was wrong with his pickup, so he pulled out the AC ducts from the dash looking for some rattle or something. He was excessively anxious about many things. For example, being robbed, having a fire in our house, grandkids getting hurt when they were here, weeds in the yard.

The concept of time was another challenge. For example, he would be ready an hour before his dentist appointment even though it was only five minutes away. One day he drove down to the garage where he was going to get his truck fixed at 5:00 a.m. despite the fact it did not open until 8:00 a.m. It's hard to explain, but almost every day, he was either really early or really late for something.

All of these things tended to make him angry and frustrated.

When he was in a good mood and had enough sleep, he kept busy mowing the lawn and weeding his trees. These were simple tasks that, once he got started, he could accomplish without assistance. Those were the good days.

On the last Sunday in March 2006, Donny had a spell of a headache and dizziness. He staggered into the bathroom. He'd gone to bed Saturday night at 8:30. He didn't complain, but he was very tired. Other than being up to the bathroom once or twice, he slept until 1:30 Sunday afternoon. Then he was then up for about five hours and was back in bed until Monday morning. He seemed to be back to his normal self.

The big picture was that he had huge mood swings, slept excessively, had short term memory issues and couldn't do simple tasks. He was often frustrated and angry which did not make him a real joy to live with. Despite all that, we did not have any serious problems with our everyday living. However, every day brought new challenges and it was getting scary.

The Woodcutter

Mike - July 12, 2006

Dad really enjoyed working on the Habitat for Humanity house. It's a very worthwhile program that helps families get a home of their own. The crew he worked with said that nobody worked harder than Dad. But I have been hearing that all my life. Dad seemed happiest when he was coming off a ten-hour day working in a long-sleeve coverall in the ninety degree sun tending his bees.

The latest crisis was caused when Dad agreed to help lay cement blocks for the Habitat House. He and another man laid an entire basement wall including the ones above their head. They told him he didn't need to do it. But he insisted. It's hard work for a thirty year old man, but physically dangerous for a seventy year old like Dad.

Since then he has experienced extreme back pain. He has a difficult time walking, especially when he has to lift his foot more than an inch or two. So when I got the call from Mom on Monday after the long 4th of July week saying that Dad needed to talk to me about getting his things in order, I drove home.

When I got to his house, we went to his shed. Dad has always had this feeling that he can see value in things that others can't. For example, he picked up a three-foot 2x4 and said it could be used for something someday. Another example was some old fence posts that he'd gotten somewhere. I thought that we'd purged him of most of his "valuables" at the auction sale, but apparently he managed to find some new ones.

We started trying to put together a list of who should get what once Dad "croaks." He didn't use the word, die, maybe croak sounded more tolerable. Kind of like, "A frog croaks all the time, so it shouldn't be a big deal for me either."

Anyway, he said that when he croaks, he wants someone to know where all the stuff should go. I told him that he wasn't going anywhere. Then I agreed that there was a good chance he would die someday, but it wasn't going to be for a while. He said he just wanted the list. So we talked about random things in the shop like pieces of board, old cabinets, a saw, a boat and an air compressor. But I think he just wanted to have someone acknowledge that his stuff had value. And that it wouldn't all just get thrown in the dumpster when he dies.

As we walked around, he seemed to want to pick up each thing and show it to me. Some of the things were heavy. He was picking them up even though he could barely touch his toes. It was almost like he was trying to show me that he was going to push himself through the pain.

He brought up croaking several more times. I told him nobody croaks from a bad back. All they do is experience more and more pain. I was trying to get him to realize that he couldn't keep working his back the way he was.

The next day when I came back at 10:00 a.m., he had drilled a big hole in the cement floor with a half-inch drill. He had also loaded the truck to go out to check the bees. He had included a chain saw, ax, maul and wood wedge to split wood. He said he wanted to cut wood when we finished with the bees. I said that nobody cuts wood when it's 90 degrees in July and that it could wait until another day.

When we were going through the beehives, I think he felt glad that someone would take care of them. He seemed to trust that I knew what I was doing, which was a little surprising. However, he started on the other end of the row of hives and opened them himself. I told him that we should just work together. He made some comment that he just didn't think he was helping out.

Dad expressed frustration that none of the Doctors had been able to fix his back. I told him that the Doctor couldn't fix it unless

Dad would rest it and give it a chance to heal. He then reiterated his frustration with the Doctors a couple more times, but he didn't seem to see any relationship between his behavior and the problem.

I said that he needed to stay out of his shed for a couple of weeks because he couldn't help himself when he went in there. It would be one thing if he would go there and sit and sort nails or something, but he insisted on moving heavy things from one side of the shed to the other. Even when I was walking around with him and kept telling him not to lift, he kept on doing it.

Given my "extensive" knowledge of psychology (one quarter in college), I think the issue is that he lacks a purpose. When he was younger he took care of his bees and made money. At one point in his life he was very into golf and played with such devotion that Tiger Woods would have been impressed. Not that he was as good as Tiger, but he played and practiced and played and practiced and then played some more. Dad never seemed to do anything half way.

When I was fishing with him, I told him I was thinking about investing in a wind turbine. He said he would like to do something like that too. I told him that was fine, but that I thought he should help me. My impression is that when a person gets old they feel like they don't have any decisions to make that really matter. They begin to feel worthless since they're not contributing to their family or society in any way that make them feel fulfilled. I think there are plenty of people who are able to volunteer or do other things that make them feel good, but those ideas didn't appeal to Dad.

I began to feel like I had a responsibility to provide Dad with a purpose. When my Grandpa was about my Dad's age, Dad had him help work with the bees. Maybe that gave my Grandpa something that Dad is missing now. I wondered if I should I be trying to do the same thing for my Dad.

But that's silly thinking. Heck, I'm forty-three and I'm not sure what my purpose is. Determining one's purpose in life is a very personal matter and one that I think many people struggle with.

Also, I think people's purposes change as they go through life. For me to tell Dad his purpose seemed unrealistic.

The closest thing Dad had to a "purpose" seemed to be to cut, split and carry firewood into the house. I helped him and I know other friends and family also helped. A couple of times, all the wood didn't get split and I told him to hold off until I was able to help. Still he took it upon himself to split the wood with a maul. And then he wondered why his shoulder kept hurting.

I began to worry that he was going to take a more direct route to ending his life. I knew he had guns around and worried that he would shoot himself. I understood this. I've heard a number of men say something like, "I would shoot myself before I'd go to the nursing home."

I tried to tell Dad that his purpose in life was to be a good grandparent. I told him I really wanted him to see my daughters get married. But that was a long way off. He seemed to like the idea, but I think it was hard for him to embrace that as his main purpose in life. He still wanted to be more vital, more important.

In a way, I blamed Dad for not developing hobbies to exercise his brain. I thought that if he did more reading, or crossword puzzles, or something like that, it would help to keep him sharp. It probably wasn't fair to think that way. Part of it was that I want to assign blame somewhere. He was putting himself and his family through all of this. I just wanted to be mad at somebody.

Every Day Drama

Sharon

At this point in his life, Donny was happiest when he was outside working on his trees or other tasks he could handle by himself. Another example was his work on his shed. He had some large pieces of tin which he'd stashed away for future usage. He dug trenches in the hard packed ground along the backside of our sheds, inserted a piece of tin and secured it to the wall. I'm not sure if he thought he was insulating the building better or if he thought it would keep out mice and other wild critters. My children and I tried to tell him it wasn't necessary and besides it was very hot and very physical work for him and it didn't seem to be a healthy thing to do. That didn't deter him and he spent many hours on that project.

The mood swings were getting progressively more intense. On bad days, we never knew what he would do next. I could leave him alone for short periods of time, but it always made me anxious and worried.

He had spells that lasted from a half-hour and up to two hours or more. These spells occurred about every week or two. He got extremely upset about one thing or another. He got angry and very stubbornly determined to do something. Often that something was strange and inappropriate.

For example, several weeks ago, he locked himself out of his workshop and broke the door down by kicking it open. My son replaced the doorknob lock and we had several extra keys made because he was always losing or misplacing them.

The next morning, he was locked out again. I had kept one of the keys, so we used that to get it open. After that, I took a bunch of the old keys, which had accumulated over the years and threw them away. He was furious, accusing me of lying and trying to mess him up. It was already very hot and I tried to get him into the house to cool off and settle down. Instead, he decided to walk about a mile to the golf course and look for golf balls. I talked him out of that, but then he insisted mowing the lawn. Our lawn was parched dry and definitely did not need mowing. My daughter was here and she finally calmed him down and talked him into taking a nap. He slept for about an hour and woke up subdued.

He simply said, "I'm sorry." When we asked what he was sorry for, he replied, "I don't remember."

Here is another example of unusual behavior. He was obsessed with getting rid of ants in our house and he sprinkled Bee Go (very smelly stuff used to repel bees) all around the outside of the house and in the garage. I was concerned that it was poisonous, but quickly found out that it was not—just extremely irritating. Our house reeked. My son and his family were here and we were both angry with him. He got very mad at my son and me and took off in the pickup about 10 p.m. I was about to call the police when he returned after forty-five minutes. He'd been to a nearby lake to swim and clean up. He hadn't been in a lake to swim for years. The next day, he was still mad at us and refused to do anything with us.

One day, he backed the car out of the garage and ten minutes later, couldn't get it in gear to back up again. He got very frustrated, then angry. He didn't drive very much but I don't think he got lost while driving.

We own a rental house and Donny was always suspicious that the renters were wrecking the house and stealing things from us that we have in storage there. Last week, he came home with some of their things in the back of his pickup. His comment was that they took our stuff so, he could take theirs. This was totally out of character for him I called the renter who was very understanding and we told him that we would return their things.

He was still sleeping excessively and was very irritable and anxious. Dr. Johnson suggested we stop the Provigil, which was supposed to keep him more awake. Instead I think it made him more irritable and he had sharper mood swings. After discontinuing it, he still slept a lot, but was less anxious and irritable. The mood swings are his biggest problem, although there are more and more memory problems. After he has had one of his "spells," he can't remember what happened or what was said.

In the last two months he's developed a pinched nerve in his back which complicates everything. He had severe pain for a couple of weeks and just wanted to die. It's much better now, but he's unable to do many of the things he'd like to do.

It would be Funny if it weren't so Sad

Mike

As Dad progressed in his illness, he regressed in his ability to keep track of things. It got to be a running joke that his billfold might turn up anyplace. It might be in the glove compartment of his pickup, or on his dresser, or in the shop, or in any number of places where he would have set it. Eventually he had two billfolds. He probably lost one, set up another, then found the first. This is just one example of the daily drama Dad pulled Mom into.

One day I wanted to borrow a pair of gloves from Dad. In the mudroom, which was Dad's personal storage area, I found a box of gloves. The problem was that they were all for the left hand. In the back of the closet, I found another box with right hand gloves. Evidently, in his mind, he was trying to organize things in a way that made sense.

When Dad moved to town, he developed a real taste for Dairy Queen. One day I stopped at the Dairy Queen and the woman sheepishly said that my Dad had been having a banana and chocolate shake once or twice every day. It was no wonder he was putting on the pounds.

He seemed to lose his sense of the value of money. About this time, he purchased a newer pickup. One day, when we were riding in it, he told me he was thinking about buying a pickup with a full extended cab. He had neither the need nor the money to be buying a new pickup. But he obsessed on things like that. If only he could get this thing or that thing, his life would be more complete.

I saw that Dad was vulnerable and I worried that people would take advantage of him. One time when I came home, Dad showed me his new knee-high hunting boots. Dad said the guy at the store told him that was what people were wearing. He was also thinking about buying a different cross bow. I went to the sporting goods store with Dad and I kind of huffed about, trying to make sure the owner knew there was someone watching over him. But the store owner didn't show any remorse, so maybe he was treating Dad right all along.

Cards

During this time we tried to play cards with Dad. In our family, everyone plays cards. Maybe it's because we're Norwegian and want to avoid the burden of making conversation, but our family holidays usually involve sitting around tables playing cards. Not mindless games of chance, but games where you have to think. Every kid learns quickly that when you're going low in Whist, you lead with your highest card in your shortest suit. If you don't know, somebody will always tell you when you screw up.

Dad had always been a good card player. So when we played and he forgot the basics and didn't follow suit or forgot what trump was, it was hard not to be mad at him. Sometimes I felt like he was just being lazy. One time I pointed out his mistakes and he got up and left the table. It made me feel like an idiot. I began to realize that it was senseless to try to argue or reason with somebody in my Dad's situation. You won't ever convince them to "try harder," and they will just feel stupid and withdraw.

Entertainment

Because we knew Mom was stuck at home with Dad, we started buying presents that we thought would help him make the time pass faster. One year for Christmas, I bought him the John Wayne movie series. Mom said he liked them, though not as much as when he was younger. I'm not sure why he didn't love them and watch them over and over again, but that's just one of the many mysteries of the disease.

Dad did get into watching documentaries. One day he watched a show on extraterrestrial life. Later that day, Dad was looking up at the sky and told Mom that "they" were watching us and would be coming again soon. He had lost his ability to distinguish between human reality and TV reality.

One day Mom took Dad to Wal-Mart. Dad went to use the bathroom. After about ten minutes, Mom started to get worried. All of a sudden Dad came flying out of the bathroom. He said they were taking pictures in there and they'd better get moving. Later, Mom figured out that he'd probably leaned forward while on the toilet and the auto flush had kicked on. She said that she giggled her way around the whole store as they shopped.

Dad's last golfing experience was pretty fun. Mom, my wife, Karen, Dad and I went to try a new golf course by Alexandria. Before every shot, we had to tell Dad where to stand and where to aim. He'd hit the ball and by the time it was his turn again, we had to tell him where to stand and where to aim. It was one of those days when he was in good humor and he just went along with it.

Mr. Social

There were times when Dad became very outgoing. One time we went to dinner at a Japanese steak house where they chop up the food in front of you. Then before your eyes, they cook it on a hot stove. The hostess put a young couple at our table with us. Dad talked and talked. He told them all about his bees and asked them lots of questions as well. About six months later, I got a call from Mom saying that the couple had stopped to visit Dad at the farm and he gave them a big tour.

It was common for him to stop and talk with people in a bar or restaurant. He was always pretty outgoing, especially when he had a couple beers in him. But once I had to guide him to our table at a restaurant because he'd sat himself down with another couple who had no idea who he was. As he became less able to recognize people or remember their names, he became even friendlier with everyone. I think he did that to cover up for the fact that he didn't remember them.

As the disease progressed, this behavior became more of a challenge for Mom and us kids. We just wanted to have a normal night out and having to keep an eye on Dad all the time made it abnormal. Maybe it shouldn't have been a big deal, a kind of harmless fun, but it was a big deal for us.

Part of it was our own vanity. One time Mom said that she figured everyone in town was talking about Dad, so we tried not to give them more to talk about.

Social Anxiety

The general trend, however, was that he was withdrawing from people. One time, some friends from Colorado were visiting for a three-day visit. Dad decided to get up at 6:00 a.m. on the second day to go work on the bees. There was nothing urgent that needed to be done, but I think Dad just wanted to get away.

Another time Dad went to the golf course one evening with a bunch of men for a steak fry. At this point, Mom appreciated getting any time to herself and she had been happy he was getting out. I asked Dad about it and he said he didn't think he'd go again. He said they were great guys and he had a great time, but he just didn't want to go again.

I am not sure why he was Mr. Social sometimes and other times he didn't want to participate in things like a steak fry with men he'd been socializing with for years. I think the circle of friends that he wanted to spend time with was getting smaller.

One day his old neighbors from the farm came to visit. They talked about how the new owner of Dad's farm was disputing a property line. The dispute had nothing to do with Dad, but he got really worked up. Mom felt terrible because the neighbors were just trying to be friendly and bring him some news. But the effect was so negative. Then you started to wonder, should we let him isolate himself? Should we ask visitors to stay away from certain subjects? Is sheltering Dad in his best interest? Should Dad have to work his way through these issues as best he can?

Personal Grooming

I've seen Dad naked many times. One of the last times was when we were staying overnight at the deer shack and Dad decided he should sit around naked with the guys. I made some joke about Dad trying to get in touch with his hairy man and then tried to rush him off to get dressed. I would put that in his bizarre behavior folder.

I remember Grandma chastising Grandpa about not shaving. She said his whiskers were white and he looked one hundred years old. It seemed that Grandpa had lost interest in personal hygiene. It became a battle to get Dad to shower and shave as well.

One Saturday afternoon, Mom wanted me to take care of Dad so she could have a break. Helping Dad undress, use the toilet, get into the shower, shampoo his hair, wash his body and then dry himself off with a towel was disturbing. It reminded me of taking care of my daughters when they were small. He, like my daughters, felt no feelings of embarrassment or shame in their nakedness, or in being told what to do. In fact, he seemed to appreciate the help.

At the basic physical need level, a person with dementia reverts back to being like a baby. They need to be fed and have their diaper changed. The difference is that I'm a lot more willing to do it for my children than my parent because my children are young and have their whole lives in front of them. My parent, however, was never going to recover and his needs kept growing.

Superman

Mike – August 2006

Dad has always possessed superman strength. I suppose every kid thinks that, but not every kid's Dad was captain of his football team, wrestling team and went to state in track. Dad was always stronger and faster. I remember in 9th grade, when I was a distance runner in track (before I realized I was a "weight man"), I thought I was in pretty good shape. So I got Dad to race me down to the road sign one-fourth of a mile away and back. He ran in his leather work boots and me in my track shoes. He beat me by a mile.

Even the way he goofs around seems to reflect that he thinks he's still a superman. He:

> ➢ "Pretended" to lift up the front of his friend's golf cart with two people in it, when we took him out golfing this summer.
> ➢ "Pretended" he was going to kick this guy he knows in the golf pro shop in the knee, but then said "I would probably just fall over anyway".
> ➢ Encouraged his granddaughters to hit him in the stomach to see how hard his stomach was.

When Dad was young he worked hard and he demanded the same of his kids. There were many times I resented having to work as much as I did. My kids are sick to death of hearing about how I worked six days a week all summer and felt lucky to get Sundays off. But on the other hand I developed a strong work ethic and that was a good thing.

Over the last year, Dad has helped me build my cabin. But it seems that he can't work like a man anymore. For example, we were putting in a lawn at the cabin and using his rototiller to prepare the ground. He wanted to run the machine for a while. I had been doing it all morning, so I said, "Sure." After about thirty minutes, I took over again. I looked at him and he was about to fall over. I walked him to the truck to sit down and got him some water. I'm sure he would have passed out otherwise.

Another time, we were cutting trees down and clearing brush. He was supposed to go sit down, but instead took the chain saw and cut down one of the good trees that we had agreed to save. I got mad and told him to sit down. I had rented a bobcat and was paying by the hour, so I went back to work. When I looked around, in his anger, he had decided to walk home. I drove around looking for him on the road but couldn't find him. It turns out that he tried to walk through someone's private property and they told him to turn around and get out.

On Memorial Day of this year, he decided that he wanted to cut wood, even though it was ninety degrees out. He tackled the biggest tree, one that blew over in the storms last year. After a couple of attempts to cut the biggest fattest part of the tree, he got the saw bound up super tight. I had to use another saw to get it loose. I was mad at him and told him he should not be doing this on a day like today.

The irony is that the man who worked so hard and made his kids work so hard, is no longer able to work at all. The thing that was most important to him was taken away.

The problem is that there is a serious disconnect between reality and his view of reality. In his mind, he is still physically strong–superman. He still thinks he can walk farther than anybody, when in fact his body is not in very good shape. He has had both knees replaced, his shoulder has been bad for years and he has a bad back. Besides, he doesn't exercise or walk much. But in his mind, he's still superman.

Death Wish

Sometimes I think Dad is trying to work himself to death.

- ➢ Dad would go to work in his bee yard when it was very hot. The guy who owns the land told me that sometimes it seemed my Dad was there a long time and came out looking very white.
- ➢ For the past several years one of his ongoing projects has been to dig up the gravel around his shed, put boards down under grade and then put gravel back. I don't think there is any logical reason for the boards and I have told Dad that, but he seems to think it will keep it from rotting. But digging out that compressed gravel is not an easy task.
- ➢ The way he kept doing things to hurt his back when he should have known to take it easy.

My guess is that on numerous times Dad has fainted or passed out from the heat while working alone. It seems he has a death wish. He wants to work so hard that he has a heart attack or falls over dead.

Protection from One's Self

So what can we do to protect Dad from Dad? He is a 230 pound grown man who is still pretty strong so he can't be physically restrained easily. And even if we could, that wouldn't be a good solution. So we have to come up with ways to get him to want to do the right thing. Maybe it's like a twelve step program where the first step is to admit you have a problem. If we could get Dad to admit that the things he's doing are not only hurting him, but hurting others around him, then he might be willing to try to change.

I feel like we are watching a slow-motion train wreck. He's unable to take care of himself. But it's not practical to have constant supervision of his activities and even if it were possible, it's doubtful that person could change his behavior. I know that I couldn't get him to stop lifting things in the shop and I'm his son.

So it seems like he's headed for more problems. Until and unless he's willing to make a change, it will be one crisis after another. I am not sure he's able to change; he may be incapable of thinking rationally. It's like yelling at a blind man to hurry up and identify the colors of the rainbow. They just have no way of understanding the question or answering even if they wanted to.

The Downhill Slide

Sharon - August 24, 2006

We were in Rochester again on Aug. 2 and 3……and, as yet, no written report. They discontinued the Namenda. Apparently it's not doing any good. They started Donny on Seroquel 25 mg three times a day for his mood swings. After two doses, he was like a zombie, so I stopped it. Now, when he gets very agitated, I give him one and a half hour later, he is ready for a nap. The doctors at Mayo could definitely see a deterioration of his mental ability.

They also told him he should not drive anymore. Although I was concerned about how he's take that news, it has been going better than I thought it would. Every now and then, he talks about driving, but he has not made any attempt to do it. I don't think he would remember now how to start any vehicle.

He gets severely depressed and talks about jumping off a cliff, or he asks me what would be the best way to end his life. The next day, everything can be fine again, but it's a roller coaster.

We still own his parents' house, where he grew up, which we have been renting out. The renters are leaving sometime this fall and he has said many times that he plans to move there. Just this morning, he told me that he should take a car out there, park in the woods until they leave, and then move into the house.

I don't feel like I can leave him for more than a couple of hours at a time. There is no way he could live by himself.

Power of Attorney

Sharon – September 2006

I decided that I needed to get legal control of the situation. My daughter, Sara and her daughter, Soffia, went with Donny and me to the attorney's office to sign the papers. Donny was so preoccupied with showing off Soffia, he laughed and signed all the papers necessary for me to have the Power of Attorney. He said that I took care of those things anyway.

I Need Help

Sharon – December 2006

My children talked me into starting home health aide visits for Donny. We have long-term care insurance and it required ninety visits before the insurance would start covering his care. Thank goodness we started the home visits when we did as nursing home care is very expensive. And thank goodness we had long-term care insurance!

It actually worked out very well to have a home health aide come three times a week to help him with a shower and getting him dressed. It had become a battle for me to get him in the shower as he always wanted to do it later. When the aide started coming, he knew it was time to shower and would take off all his clothes when he saw her drive in the yard. I was a bit concerned that he might make sexual advances to her because he certainly had no inhibitions in being nude when she came. I talked to her about it and she assured me she knew how to handle him and could take care of herself. She was an absolute angel.

I also utilized a respite person several times so I could get away for an afternoon of bridge or whatever. He never liked the respite people as well as the home health aide, but it did help me get away occasionally.

Dinner Party to Forget

Sharon – December 2006

Trying to maintain some normalcy in my life, I had guests over for dinner. Donny had a bathroom urge while we were eating and left the table. After a few minutes, I checked on him and found him– and everything in the bathroom– smeared with poop: the stool, the sink, the floor, the shower curtain and the wall. You get the picture. The guests had already starting eating and I told them to continue and I'd be right back. I then tried to clean up the bathroom and Donny. And I was looking for some normalcy.

Obviously it was a very unpleasant and uncomfortable situation for us and our guests. I knew it was our last dinner party.

Another strange event happened during that Christmas season. Mike and his family were here and he and I left for a while to take care of some business. Karen, my daughter in law, was home with Donny and some grandkids. Donny went into the bedroom, shut the door and was very quiet. Karen assumed he was taking a nap and everyone else was watching TV. When I got home, I went in to check on him. He was sitting on the edge of the bed and with a sharp pocket knife was cutting his heavy hunting socks into one inch strips and tying the strips together. When I asked what he was doing, he just got up and left the room. Crazy behavior, but it did teach us to remove all sharp pocket knives and guns from the house.

Thank goodness my children have been very supportive during this difficult time. For a while now, they have arranged their schedules so that at least one of them can be here every weekend.

Alzheimer's Memory Walk

Mike – October 2006

Thank You, for giving from the heart

We decided to participate as a family in the local Alzheimer's Memory Walk. We collected pledges and raised several thousand dollars. Some of the people I work with were going to be there and I was a little nervous about them meeting my Dad.

Dad, however, was not worried about being looked at like a patient. We told him we were there to honor his Dad and he was fine with that. There were activities there for the grandkids and the atmosphere was quite festive, like a carnival. Even the Minnesota Vikings cheerleaders were there. My Dad was not self-conscious about his disease. I don't think he had much self-awareness. I doubt he thought the walk had anything to do with him, personally, other than that he and his family were walking.

Dad was excited to be able to push the baby stroller. So he pushed it the entire 1.7 mile length of the walk. As we were nearing the end, I noticed that he was walking by himself. He tried to turn off the walk into a parking lot but an attendant waved him back to the path. I caught up with him and noticed that he was sweating profusely and walking a little hunched over.

Sometimes, especially when he's tired, Dad walks like a ninety-year-old man. He hunches over and shuffles his feet. Until yesterday, I hadn't really noticed it, but from now on, it will be something to watch for.

I began pushing the stroller so Dad could just walk more easily. We came to a sidewalk next to another parking lot and he walked off the curb and fell down. It was not a graceful fall. He took a couple of steps on his way down and he landed on the pavement with his hands in front of him.

Many people saw this entire episode transpire and of course the first thing that jumped into my mind was to get him up so we don't create a scene. I wish I could say that my first concern was his health, but at that point, it wasn't. Sorry about that God.

Then he put his hands out to me and asked me "to lift up his fingers." I don't know why he said "fingers," but that's what he said. I tried to pull him up by pulling on his hands, but couldn't. A man in the crowd said, "Take it easy," and I suppose he was right, but at the time I felt I was trying to help Dad get up in the way he wanted. Finally Dad rolled over and got up, looking like a hundred-year-old man.

He was bleeding on his both his hands and his cheek. I took him to the bathroom and we washed up as much as we could. Then we then went to the first aid stand and they put some bandages on his cuts and scratches. The carnival was over. Afterwards, Dad slept most of the afternoon.

Coming to a Head

Sharon - December 26, 2006

Donny has definitely deteriorated in the last couple of months. He's unable to do even the simplest tasks without direct supervision. He can dress by himself, but it's usually inappropriate–such as putting on three pair of briefs, two T-shirts and three stockings on each foot. Minor things, really, but when we're going someplace, I need to help him every step of the way.

The more serious, immediate problem is his frequent and urgent need to urinate and the last few days, he's complained of burning. He seldom makes it to the bathroom without wetting himself to some degree. Twice, he's been incontinent of his stools, both times making a terrible mess. The first time, there was stool all over our bathroom and him. Last Saturday night, sometime during the night, it happened again. Besides soiling both bathrooms and dropping stool on our dining room carpet, he went outside in only his T-shirt and briefs barefoot. It was about ten degrees above zero that day after Christmas and Donny left a good sized deposit of stool on our deck. He made it back to bed, but in the process, soiled our sheets and our bedding. In the morning, he remembered only that his feet had gotten really cold.

There have been three times that he hasn't known me. Once, he thought I was his mother and asked me where Sharon was. I thought I had heard wrong and asked him to repeat what he'd said and he repeated the same thing.

He fell again this afternoon (Tuesday). I know of six or seven falls in the last two months. Most of the falls have been outside,

61

but once he fell face forward going down the steps. He has complained about a pain in his right wrist but I don't think it is serious.

Respite in Hawaii

Sharon – February 2007

I had initially planned to take Donny with me to stay at my brother's rental place in Hawaii. But after the Christmas Eve episode of him having incontinent stool all over my house and out on the deck, I decided it wouldn't work to take him with us. I arranged for him to stay at an adult foster home and he actually seemed relieved that he didn't have to travel. He seemed to be fine about staying there. He apparently did fine there at first and, was cooperative, ate well and was helpful with household errands. But on a snow stormy afternoon, unnoticed by the staff, he walked out of the house. He had on a light jacket and was wearing one tennis shoe and carrying the other one. He walked in the heavy snow with just a stocking on the one foot. It was blizzard conditions and Donny was picked up by a man driving a snowplow. The man notified the police and was told to bring him to the hospital to be checked over for frost bite or any other injuries. Donny told the E.R. personnel that he was just trying to get home. Donny didn't have frostbite or any other physical problems and was returned to the adult foster home until I returned home. When I was called in Hawaii, I felt helpless and sad about the whole affair.

Doctor, can you help us?

Sharon – March 14, 2007

This is a note I wrote to give to Donny's doctor so I would not have to say it in front of him:

"I am concerned about Donny's physical condition.... He shuffles more, has tremors and just does not look well. His eyes are slightly bloodshot and not clear. His pacemaker has checked out fine. After even on a short walk, he has very labored respirations and has to rest. And then there are other times when he can walk much more and it doesn't bother him at all. Other than his shoulder and wrist, he has not complained about any pain.

Mentally, he is irrational almost all of the time. He does remember things, but it's more of a behavior problem. He needs help dressing, bathing, toileting and supervision in eating. He cannot follow simple instructions. He sleeps a lot. There are days when he is really ornery and does not want to do anything. Taking his pills has been a daily challenge. At times, he is very depressed and just wants to die. I don't think he would do anything intentionally to hurt himself.

Are we okay with his medications, or is there anything else that might help?"

From Bad to Worse

Mike

As Dad's condition deteriorated, we were concerned about what the next steps would be for his care. His long-term care policy would pay for home care, but only after we paid for ninety home-care visits or nursing home days. For some reason, we didn't start the home-care visits as soon as we could. Our late start was partly due to the fact that we didn't want to acknowledge that Dad was getting worse or that Mom needed help.

We finally started with home care in December 2006. Even in a small town, I never realized the number of resources that were available. A lady came into the house, gave Dad a shower, shave and got him dressed in clean clothes. That could take two to three hours. It was a real relief to Mom to be able to get out of the house for short periods of time. In retrospect, we should have started having some form of home care much earlier than we did.

The home care was great. I think it enabled Dad to stay at home longer and maybe prevented Mom from having a nervous breakdown. In January 2007, Dad and I went snowmobiling. Dad drove his own snowmobile and we went all over the county. We stopped and had a beer and just had a good time. Little did I imagine that in less than a year, he would be unable to walk and would be a nursing home.

Group Home

Mom wanted to go to Hawaii for three weeks with her siblings in February. It was obvious that taking Dad was not realistic nor would he want to go. Therefore, we decided to have him stay in a group home. It was really just a big house, about three miles out of town, which had a big living room and some extra bedrooms. It was a locked facility and the home had some form of certification which enabled them to take in people like Dad for so much per day. The idea was that Dad would stay there while Mom was gone and then go back with Mom when she got home.

I remember one time I stopped and picked him up on a Saturday afternoon. I also got Grandma from the nursing home. The three of us went out for a drive. I had been doing this with them for a while. We drove around the old neighborhood and I tried to get them talking about the people in their lives. After a while, we'd get some chicken from A&W, then sit and eat at Mt Lookout. Grandma thought this was great fun. Dad, on the other hand, could be a little difficult. Maybe it was because I had done it once too many times, but on this trip he said, "Not another car ride!"

One night, back in Bloomington, I got a phone call from Alan Braaten, a family friend. He told me that they had picked up Dad walking along the highway half way between the group home and Glenwood. It was cold and windy and I think the wind chill was below zero. I don't know all the details, but I think he just had on pajamas. He maybe just had stockings on his feet.

Alan said that Dad was at the hospital and I was supposed to call there. I called and explained that he was my Dad, my Mom was out of the state and that he had been staying at a group home. I'm not sure if it was their normal professional skepticism, but I felt like they were wondering what kind of family would let this happen to a poor defenseless man.

Finally, they put him on the phone. I tried to talk to him, but he didn't respond. The nurse took the phone back. I called the group home and they said they'd already been told he was at the hospital. She said they didn't know how he could have gotten out of the house because it was locked. She apologized up and down, then said she would pick him up and bring him back to the house.

I wasn't sure if I should call my Mom or not. I didn't want to ruin her vacation, but, on the other hand, I thought she should hear about it from me instead of someone else. So I called her in Hawaii and told her what had happened. We agreed there was nothing she could do and she might as well finish her vacation.

Back Home

When Mom got back from Hawaii, she took Dad back to the house with her. But there were plenty of daily struggles. I don't think anybody understands what a spouse has to endure unless they go through it themselves. The spouse is always sitting on pins and needles, waiting for the next crisis.

At this stage in his life, I wondered about Dad's quality of life. On the plus side he was living at home and every once in a while there would be a flash of the man he used to be. But most of the time he did not seem happy. He did not really want to talk much and we kind of had to drag conversation out of him. He often seemed frustrated.

The turning event happened in April. Early one morning Mom was trying to get Dad dressed or something and Dad pulled back his arm like he was going to hit her. From that point on, Mom felt threatened. Dad had crossed a line. This was the beginning of the worst year.

The Worst Year

Sharon - Sunday morning, April 15, 2007, at 4 a.m.

Donny became very belligerent, very angry and balled up his fist
and drew it back to hit me. I looked him in the eye and, as calmly
as I could, said, "You don't want to do that." He slowly lowered
his fist. He had taken his diaper off and was totally uncoopera-
tive. He wouldn't put another diaper on after having a BM in bed
and dribbling all the way to the bathroom. We walked around the
house for about an hour and he was trying to destroy whatever he
could get his hands on. He finally got tired and I took him back
to bed.

In the morning, I called Dr. Schluter and asked him to admit
Donny to the hospital. Dr. Schluter said he couldn't do that.
He said the hospital was not equipped to care for such cases
and he couldn't subject the nursing staff to violent behavior.
I was upset about what had happened and pressed him for a
recommendation.

The doctor said to give him three Risperdal pills for sedation.
If I couldn't manage him after that, he would find a placement
for him. He suggested a facility in Litchfield where they treat
adults with behavior problems. The pills knocked him out for
a short nap and when he woke, he was in a much better mood.
The doctor told me to increase his pills to two in the morning
and one at night, which I have done. He has not been belligerent since. He makes no sense in what he is talking about and
doesn't know what's going on. He is incontinent of both stool
and urine now. He knows he has to go, but doesn't know where

69

he should go. He usually doesn't get there in time and needs help once there.

As a nurse, I don't feel particularly proud of the fact that we are using drugs to subdue him, but what choice do I have?

Several adult foster homes told me this morning that they wouldn't be able to safely have him in their facility because of his high risk for wandering and belligerent behavior. I wasn't surprised and I agreed with their decision.

Decision Made

Sharon – April 17, 2007

When Donny threatened me, it was the beginning of a new phase of his disease. We had been managing with the help of Home Health services and some volunteer respite services since before Christmas. Incontinence of both urine and bowel was an increasing problem, but even that was tolerable until he threatened me. Donny did not threaten me again in a sedated state, but I pursued placement for him in a behavioral and medication evaluation facility.

Litchfield

Sharon – April 20, 2007

Donny was accepted at a specialized unit at Meeker County Memorial Hospital. I told him that I was taking him to a hospital that could help him. He had no objections and got into the car willingly. My daughter met us at the hospital and that was helpful for both Donny and me. I was feeling like a failure in the role of caregiver. As a nurse, I should have been able to handle him. I think I also felt that other people thought less of me, but maybe that was just in my own head.

I told the psychiatrist about his violent outburst and his comment was that if he did it once, he would do it again and the episodes would be more frequent. Very prophetic!

The hospital had a unit that specialized in adult behavior problems, usually involved in some sort of dementia. Their policy was to keep a person for a minimum of ten days to fully evaluate their medications and their behavior. They immediately discontinued the medications he was on and started their own regime-primarily lithium, Prozac and Ambien. He was a model patient and I had the feeling that the staff wondered why he was there. Toward the end of the ten days, we were making arrangements for him to live in an adult assisted living facility in Alexandria, a place close to our home.

The plan was to discharge him from Litchfield on Monday, April 30th and move him to a locked adult foster home in Alexandria. When I came to pick him up, he was belligerent and angry, refusing food and medications. We had a conference call with the Alexandria facility and they were willing to take him, but the Litchfield staff was skeptical because of his drastic change of behavior. The staff in Alexandria was confident that they could handle him and that he would settle down once he got settled in a home-like atmosphere. We finally decided to transfer him as he had calmed down some. I got him to take his pills and off we went. The ride was uneventful. We had lunch together when we got there and I was hopeful that it would be a good placement for Donny. He had always been an outdoors type of person and after being indoors for several weeks at Litchfield, he could now be outside in a safe area and receive good care inside. I was very thankful that there are places like this home.

Alexandria

He did very well the first two weeks in Alexandria. He was helpful with kitchen chores, helped plant and weed flowers and spent time sorting nuts and bolts. The third week, on a Tuesday, I had lunch with him and he was very agitated. He couldn't express his feelings with me, or visit with me about things at home or about our family. He didn't appear to be angry at me, but kept moving from one place to another showing me the nuts and bolts he was working on and where the TV was. He couldn't focus on any one activity and paced around the house. Later, the staff members told me he deteriorated from that point on. Maybe I triggered the onset of deterioration. I'm not sure how, but maybe I did.

On Friday, the facility called and said he had refused his pills and his food and was agitated. An hour later, they called again and said he had fallen and was at the Douglas County Hospital emergency room getting stiches in his ear. The facility did not want to take him back, but because there was no place to take him, they were obligated to take him.

Two days later, he kicked over a garbage can, picked up a chair, threw it at the wall and started swinging his arms at one of the staff. The staff called for an ambulance, but the police came first and put him in handcuffs. Because he had "attacked" someone, this was "their policy." By the time the police got there, the staff told me that he was calm and cooperative and went with the police willingly. He did not go by ambulance. How humiliating that must have been for him. I was angry with the police involvement and especially that they had put him in handcuffs. The staff was also very upset that the police acted the way they did and they wrote a letter of protest to the city, but nothing ever came of that.

This event happened on a Sunday afternoon and now the assisted living facility absolutely refused to take him back. He sat in the emergency room for most of the afternoon while they searched for a place for him to go. Litchfield had no room and most facilities of that nature do not take Sunday admissions. The only option was a state mental health facility in Wadena. I was in telephone contact with the hospital during this time, feeling anxious and concerned about what was going to happen next. They kept telling me not to come to the hospital because he would be transferred as soon as possible. They finally informed me that the sheriff's department was taking him to Wadena and that I should go there in the morning. I never asked if they put him in hand-cuffs again, but I knew he was sedated.

Wadena

The Wadena facility was a locked unit and I had to leave all my personal belongings in a locker. When I got inside the unit, I again became angry and very upset. It definitely was not a place for people with dementia. With all that I been through up to this point, it didn't take much to disturb me. I felt completely overwhelmed and trapped in a helpless, hopeless situation.

Donny had received a lot of sedation at the Alexandria hospital and when he received his regular medication on top of that, he was overdosed–incoherent and barely functional. He has always been intolerant to medication and had reacted adversely to many meds. It was his history. He hadn't been shaved for several days and was sitting in a chair drooling–a very depressing sight

While I was there doing admission paperwork, he was cleaned, shaved and became more alert. They were very up front with me about the fact that this was not the place for Donny. The residents of this facility were young to middle age adult males who either had mental illness or drug and alcohol problems. I could hear the anger in their voices as they were pacing around the great room. I also witnessed a potential physical confrontation between two men that was diffused by a staff member. There were no males there that had dementia and the doctor said he wasn't competent in treating that disease. He had contacted the doctor in Litchfield and ordered the same drugs that he'd been given there. The whole atmosphere of potential and actual violence was very scary and certainly did not make me feel comfortable, either for myself or for Donny.

Litchfield was reluctant to take him back, but finally said they would when they had room. Because a person cannot be held in a state mental health facility for more than seventy-two hours, I needed to be declared his legal guardian to request that he stay in

Wadena. It was obvious that Donny was incapable of making any decisions and I was not a guardian. I was told to contact my lawyer to get an emergency guardianship effective immediately, which I did. If Litchfield couldn't take him within that seventy-two hour time frame, I would need that guardianship to keep him in the Wadena facility.

I got the necessary papers to be an emergency guardian and later had to appear before a judge to make it permanent. That too, was an intimidating experience. The court appointed a lawyer to represent Donny and I had my lawyer present for the hearing. It seemed odd that there would be two sides arguing a case when, in my mind, there was not two sides to argue. I just wanted to do what was right for Donny. I didn't know if I would be questioned about why he had been in Wadena, or questioned about his medical condition. It was an unknown situation for me and made me very nervous. It was also very sad. The hearing was over quickly and turned out to be pretty uneventful.

I returned to Wadena the next day with the emergency guardianship papers in hand. There was a care conference scheduled and it would give me a chance to talk to the psychiatrist in charge. It was not a good scene. When I walked into the unit, I was told that Donny was refusing food, medications, personal care and was just plain ornery. He had a determined, angry look on his face when I entered his room, which he had refused to leave. There was a male attendant with him to protect him from himself and to prevent him from harming others. I helped calm him down and got him to eat some food. We were still waiting for word from Litchfield.

The care conference was an eye opener. The psychiatrist said that this was a totally wrong placement for Donny as this facility was for mentally ill males and not for older, male dementia patients. He admitted that he was not qualified or capable of handling Donny's medications and deferred back to notes from the Litchfield facility. They also wanted him transferred ASAP because of the seventy-two hour hold.

That evening, I got a call saying that a medi-van would transfer him to Litchfield the next day. I was relieved to get him out of

Wadena, but unsure of what the future held in store for us. I no longer needed to be his guardian, but kept it in case I needed it later.

Back to Litchfield

Donny was returned to Litchfield (MCMH) on Thursday, May 24th. I went there on Friday and was surprised to find him in a very good mood. Everything was very funny, inappropriately so, but the visit made me feel relieved. I thought things were looking better, but the honeymoon didn't last.

His second stay in Litchfield was traumatic and heart wrenching for us as a family. It's hard to remember the sequence of events and maybe I even tried to forget some of them.

He began having violent outbursts and ended up spending several nights in the "secured" room—a locked room with a mattress, pillow and blanket–and with a toilet. They tried many different medications, different doses and have had poor results. One morning, he got diaphoretic—pale and sweaty, with labored breathing. Another day, a "normal" dose of sedative (Ativan 2 mg) knocked him out for six hours. When I visited on Thursday, May 30th, he was in tough shape. He couldn't walk without help, couldn't eat without help, did not know me and was totally disoriented. He didn't know my name, but said I was a nice lady. When talking to the nurse, she looked up the side effects to his drugs and found that he had classic symptoms of every known side effect there was. So, all the drugs were discontinued and, after two days, a new regime was started.

He became more alert and was able to walk, but his behavior became more aggressive. One Sunday afternoon late in May, he hit an older female resident in the forehead without being provoked. The lady needed stitches for a cut, but had no broken bones. I received a tearful, hysterical telephone call from the nurse on duty screaming at me to get him out of there and that he was in the locked security room for the night. My daughter and her husband were in route back to Maple Grove and when I told her what had happened, they made a side trip to Litchfield. By the time they arrived, Donny had calmed down and my daughter talked and prayed with him.

When I got there the next day, Donny was very mellow and apologetic. He knew he had hit someone and was remorseful. The male aide that had spent the night with him was very kind to Donny and said that he knew Donny was not a mean person and just did not realize what he was doing. I appreciated that.

On Monday, June 11, 2007, I received another bad telephone call. Donny had a grand mal seizure that morning and was not regaining consciousness. The doctor called about five minutes later and said that Donny was having labored breathing and they feared he had had a massive stroke. They didn't think he would recover. I left immediately and Sara was able to get away from work to meet me there. By the time I got to Litchfield, I had mentally prepared his funeral. I knew what day it would be, what we would have for lunch and thinking about who I would have to call. He was asleep when we got there and was resting peacefully. The CAT scan had not shown any massive stroke as we were told, so it was a wait-see situation. By the middle of the afternoon, he began waking up and by evening was walking around showing no after effects of the seizure. The seizure had lasted about five minutes and in a different person would probably have caused death. It's my belief that his pacemaker kept him alive.

Sunday, June 17th, was Father's Day and Donny's 71st birthday. Two of my sons and my daughter arranged to have dinner with him in an attempt of a celebration. He was pretty quiet while we were there, but did talk some and walked with us to a private room for dinner. He ate by himself with minimal assistance and later danced his way back to his room. It was a glimmer of his old self and we all had a good laugh. It was nice that we could all be together, but a bittersweet day.

By the end of the week, I was told that he was ready for discharge to another facility. They resumed his medications with the addition of Dilantin, which is given to prevent any further seizures and he had no further behavior outbursts.

Cosmos

I visited nursing homes and assisted living facilities closer to home, but no one would take him because of his history of behavior outbursts. Litchfield would not keep him so once again there was a panic about finding a place for him to go. Thankfully, a nurse who worked at Litchfield part time was also the manager of an assisted living facility in Cosmos, MN. She was willing to take him when no one else would and he was transferred there on June 19th.

When he went to Cosmos, he was able to walk, talk and feed himself with some help. He seemed to make some friends and, generally, was well behaved. One day when I stopped, he was obviously overmedicated again. One of the characteristics of frontal lobe dementia is that the person is very sensitive to medications. This was certainly true with Donny and I had seen it many times before. I told them to hold all of his meds until he woke up. I had to go to the top of the ladder of authority to do it, but they did it reluctantly. It took him about ten days to become more alert again and then they just gave him the Dilantin for seizure prevention. He did not have any more behavior outbursts and did not need any behavior modification med other than Ativan for sleep.

Back to the Glenwood

About the middle of July, Donny seemed to stabilize in his behavior and there weren't any more problems. Cosmos was a good facility, but it was seventy-five miles from our home. I needed to find a place closer to me so I could visit him more often. I knew that soon he would require more care than an assisted living facility could give him and that he needed a nursing home. He had been in many different places and it would be better to find a permanent home for him to avoid any further confusion. I also wanted his medical care to be overseen by our family doctor since he knew Donny very well. There had been many different doctors in the last three months and they were always changing his medications. Donny needed some stability in his life and I wanted him as close to me as possible.

Mother and Son Together Again

Seeing the Sunny Side

Sharon

Sylvia was very non-judgmental and accepting of everything my family did. I know that there were times she disapproved about things happening at our house, but she never reproached us. She was also very humble and was happy with whatever she had. She didn't complain and really appreciated our visits. We'd pick her up at the GRV and bring her to someone's house for a holiday and she had the best time. Unfortunately, she had a "bathroom accident" at my brother's house which made us unwilling to take her again.

The only time she got angry with me was the day she was moved to the Rainbow Room. When I went to see her, she was livid, wild-eyed and accused me of plotting against her. It was very hurtful and both of us cried. The nursing staff told me to leave and come back later, which I did. By then she had calmed down and she never mentioned the move again. Eventually, she'd say, "I have it so good here; people are so nice." However, she did have some bouts of depression because she missed her husband, her mother and friends who were no longer alive.

Dad's Last Hunt

Not Another One

Mike

I was not excited about Dad going to the same place as Grandma. Dad, at age 71, was too young for the GRV. What would people think? "Another Larson in the GRV, pretty soon they'll need their own wing." But the more I thought about it, I realized it didn't really matter. Putting him somewhere else wasn't going to fool anybody. We might as well face up to the situation and put him somewhere convenient for Mom.

Together Again

Sharon – July 2007

I was reluctant to bring Donny to the GRV because his mother was there. He wouldn't have to be in the same unit as she was because he wasn't wandering and didn't need a quiet environment. He would be in the unit adjoining hers. I didn't think it would make any difference to Donny, but worried that it might be hard on his mother. We had not told her anything about his condition other than he wasn't feeling well. She asked about him almost every visit and seemed satisfied with answers like "He was busy," or "He was working," or "He wasn't feeling well."

GRV was concerned about his behavior history, but they agreed to take him on a trial basis. I was very open with them about his violent behavior, but told them he had not had any violent outbursts for two months. I also think the fact that we have strong ties with GRV because of other relatives being there may have influenced their decision. When I picked him up, I had a new car which I think confused him. I was able to get him into my car with a little help and uneventfully brought him home to Glenwood on July 23rd. Mike met me at GRV. We pushed his wheelchair around on the bike paths by the lake. You'd think that at this point we

80

would have all had a total meltdown, but the feeling was almost anticlimactic. I had been through many different care facilities for Donny many times already. This was one more step and, hopefully, the last one. The staff put him in the same room that my dad was when he died– that was a bit disconcerting, but logically okay.

I asked that they keep Donny and his mother apart and the staff very conscientiously did what I asked. If one was in the Chapel, they kept the other one out of there. One day when I went there, all the residents and staff were in the dining room for special music and some kind of party. Everyone but Donny was there. He was alone in the sitting room. I had asked that he eat in the sitting room because there were people in the dining room that would know him and it would be uncomfortable for me. They were keeping them separate, like I requested, but I became very angry that he was alone. I told the staff that their care was not acceptable and they'd better get their act together. In hindsight I felt bad about the way I reacted. My only excuse was that I was under a lot of the stress and turmoil. Later I did apologize.

After a week of this, I was the one having a problem with keeping them apart. I felt like I was living a lie, visiting one and then the other. I also felt bad for the staff because it put them in a difficult situation many times.

Finally, it became clear that keeping them apart was making it more stressful without producing any benefits. I decided that I had to tell Sylvia what was going on. As a mother, she had the right to know. After I told her, she shed a few tears, but then said she would like to see him soon. Donny was sound asleep that day, so I came back the next day. She was happy to see him and was very motherly towards him (she had always doted on him lovingly). She rubbed his arm and held his hand and told him that they both had to work hard at getting better. She was very brave.

He didn't respond to her at all. By then, he was talking very little, but his mother was very cheerful and upbeat while we were together. After I got Donny back to his room, I went back to her room and she was sobbing her heart out. Days later she went to chapel with him and she again held his hand and talked to him.

81

She often asked me, "Won't he ever get better?" She was a loving mother to the end.

Her Little Boy

Mike – November 2008

I visited Dad yesterday and all he did was sleep. I couldn't get him to open his eyes. Then I went to visit Grandma in the TV room. She was talkative. The Vikings game was on TV and I don't know if that got her confused, but she said she was watching Donny play football and he'd almost caught the ball. In her mind, Donny will always be her little boy catching the ball.

Grandma Passes

Mike – June 2009

We got a call that the home had not been able to wake Grandma from her afternoon nap. They couldn't reach Mom, so they moved Grandma to the hospital. My wife, daughters and I went back to Glenwood because they didn't think she would live. We stopped at the hospital on Friday evening and my daughters got to say good-bye, even though Grandma was not conscious.

The next morning I met my Mom, aunt and uncle, great uncle and sister at the hospital. We took turns sitting by her bed and standing around in the hallway. Suddenly Mom, being a nurse, noticed a change in Grandma's breathing and called for my aunt to come back from making a telephone call. My aunt was holding Grandma's hand and said, "Just let go, Mom, we love you." Grandma took one last deep breath and then died.

It was the first time I have ever been in the room when someone has died. I hope that when I die, I die as loved as she was.

My Kids Would Never put me in a Nursing Home

Mike - November 10, 2008

Norman and Marlene were close personal friends of my parents. For at least twenty-five years, they spent countless nights playing bridge. Norman had spent twenty-some years in the army on the US Rifle team. He's a gifted story teller, so he's always fun to be around.

Dad considered Norman one of his closest friends. In addition to cards, they hunted together, vacationed together and drank together. They'd known each other since they were kids and knew everything about each other. One time, when we were pheasant hunting in South Dakota, Norman had Dad hold his drink. Dad asked if Norman trusted him and Norman said that he trusted Dad with everything, including his wife and his drink. On second thought, he added, maybe not the drink.

I know that Norman visited Dad in the group home in Alexandria and maybe at the GRV, but not more than once or twice. That's the case for most of his friends. I think they must feel like I feel. I'm not sure it's doing him any good and I know dang sure it doesn't do me any good. I come away depressed and sad seeing him like that.

Marlene has been diagnosed with Alzheimer's disease. One night Norman and Marlene came to visit Mom and me. While Marlene was sitting there, Norman said that the Amoxicillin has helped, but she can't remember anything short-term. That's why,

Norman said, she wants to screw all the time. She can't remember that they just did it that morning.

Norman and Marlene have kids that have been very successful financially. Norman said something like. "My kids would never put Marlene or me in a nursing home. They are talking about building a guest house next to theirs and having full time help for us to be able to stay there."

This comment set my Mom completely off her rocker. She said, "Are you saying that we are not doing a good thing for Donny because he is in a nursing home? Do you think I was a poor spouse for not taking care of him here at home?"

Norman responded that was not at all what he meant. He has a lot of respect for what my Mom has gone through and the way she has handled things. It's just that his family might handle it differently. Not that it's necessarily better or worse, just different.

The next day Mom said she doesn't need to see Norman again. I hope she finds it in her heart to forgive him because I don't think he was being critical of her or of us.

I'll bet almost everybody has been inside a nursing home and would agree that it's the most depressing place they've ever been. I don't know of a single person who wants to be a resident of a nursing home. But I have heard several residents say something to the effect of, "I shouldn't be here; I don't know why my family put me in here."

I have personally spent way more time in nursing homes than I would ever wish on anybody. I have had a close relative there for the last twenty-five years. I am far from an expert on the matter, but I have observed that, for the most part, the care given is exemplary. The staff genuinely cares about the residents and tries to make them comfortable. The staff doesn't get paid a lot, the hours are terrible and it's hard, dirty work. I know I wouldn't like to change adult diapers.

The problem is how to provide the residents with the highest quality of life possible. Many sleep fourteen hours a day. When they are awake, many just watch TV or listen to the radio. There are puzzles, games, organized activities, outings and all kinds of things to do. But in my experience, except for the rousing bingo game with my Grandpa Joe when we won candy bars, most of the residents don't participate.

Yesterday I sat at a table with my Grandma and two other ladies, Olive and Jo. The three ladies introduced themselves to one another (even though they all live together). My Grandma asked Jo if she was on the train that morning. Of course there was no train. My Grandma probably dreamed about it or something. Jo was kind enough to say that she wasn't on the train. They tried a couple of other topics, but I think they all got frustrated and gave up. This is an example of the challenges elderly people face in keeping themselves socially involved. It's hard to have a conversation when one or more in the group are not completely in the here and now—plus, hearing is often an issue too.

It's appealing to think that if I ever required that level of care, I'd go to my own private little sanctuary where I'm the only resident. I wouldn't be surrounded by people worse than I was, or those with bad attitudes. I'd have plenty of friends, family and paid staff to keep me mentally sharp and in as peak physical condition as possible. I would have a positive outlook on life and would only see the humorous side of my declining mental and physical condition.

However, I'm not sure that's a realistic expectation. The reality is that all of us are going to die. And those of us who die at an older age are going to experience physical and mental setbacks. We are not always going to have a positive attitude. We're going to feel sorry for ourselves. And we're not going to get the recognition or number of visits we would like to have from family and friends. Where we live is probably not the determining factor in how we deal with those realities. I think it has more to do with our attitude and outlook on life.

If someone wants their own personal nursing home and they can afford it, good for them. I am not sure it will make their experience better, but to each their own.

Finding Peace

Sharon – August 12, 2007

Today was a memorable day. Paul was home from New Jersey and he had not seen his dad since last October when Donny and I went to visit him. All our children and grandchildren were here for the weekend and the grandchildren had not seen him since he was moved out of our house. I requested that we all go to church together at the chapel of GRV. There was some reluctance, but I felt it was important that all of our children and grandchildren know that we weren't abandoning their Grandpa. He's sick but he's still a part of our lives. It was a very emotional day to say the least.

Little Sylvia, age 4, was the bright spot of the day. She first crawled up on Great Grandma's lap and gave her a hug and a kiss. Then she proceeded to do the same with Donny. She perched on the wheelchair armrest between Donny and me for the rest of the service. She put her arm around him and her head on his shoulder, then stroked his arm and hand the whole time. He responded to her, trying to kiss her and rubbing her arm also. It was a beautiful scene, but of course, reduced the rest of us to tears. I will always remember it.

Uncertain Future

Sharon - October 10, 2007

We don't know what lies ahead for Donny and our family. He doesn't walk at all anymore, can't feed himself and says only occasional words that usually don't make any sense. Today, the aides told me that when they were getting him out of bed, he kept saying, "Sharon, don't. No Sharon." It was comforting to know that he still remembers my name.

Peace

Mike – November 2007

Working near Glenwood has given me the opportunity to see Dad and Grandma more often. Many nights I will hold hands with Dad and pray. We always pray for peace for Dad. Last night his roommate Jim was also there and we were talking. Jim said Dad is an easy roommate. I said I just wished Dad would find peace.

So when I left I was rubbing his shoulders and I gave him a hug and said goodbye. And I swear to God he said, "Peace to you."

Felt like a miracle that he could communicate something like that to me.

Fade to Black

Sharon - Nov. 29, 2008

Last year at this time, I couldn't think about Christmas without crying. So much had happened and I felt such a loss without my husband in my own home. At a routine doctor's visit, he asked me how I was doing and I burst into tears. He said it was time for antidepressants for me and I didn't object. It helped me get through the holidays. I initially went to the home daily, but after six-or-seven months of that, I knew I had to make fewer visits. It was getting the best of me and left me depressed.

On Wednesday afternoons at the home, they usually have some live music entertainment for the residents. On one of these days, I had both Sylvia and Donny there, with Donny sitting in the middle. They were playing some of the good old songs that we used to dance to and Donny loved to dance. Donny started to cry and his mother rubbed his arm wondering if he hurt someplace. She was trying to soothe him. It broke my heart.

Over the weeks, Donny was unable to walk and he talked less and less. When he did say anything, it was usually just a few words mumbled softly and easily missed. A few months ago when I was leaving, I gave him a kiss and told him I loved him and in a very soft mumble, he said, "I love you too." That's as good as it gets for me right now.

It's getting more and more difficult for our children and grandchildren to visit Donny. I don't insist on it anymore and re-spect their feelings. It's probably better for the older grandkids to remember him as a loving fun grandpa who would do anything for them.

I try to get in to feed Donny three to four times a week. I can't have a conversation with him and feeding him makes me feel like at least I can do something for him. I'm not sure he always knows me, but once in a while there's a spark of recognition. I'm off the anti-depressants now, but I still have some down times. It's been a tough journey for Donny so far and for our family. We don't know when or how this journey will end.

There But Not Really

Sharon – January 28, 2010

It's been two and a-half years since Donny has been in the GRV and going on three years since he has been in my home. When reading over my past notes, we are not facing the acute problems that we had in 2007. I would hate to go through anything like that again. It's still difficult, but in a different way. I'm back on the antidepressants.

When people ask about him, I tell them that he's "Just there," and is unable to walk or talk or feed himself. I don't encourage people to visit him because he's unable to visit and it's hard to know if he knows them or not. It ends up being awkward for visitors and me and I don't believe it serves any purpose for anyone.

He shows very little emotion and if awake, just stares into space. Once in a great, great while, I get a slight smile. When Sara and her two little girls come, they sometimes get a smile also. Little Lyla, now age two, likes to ride in the wheelchair and says, "Up, up," and sits in his lap for a ride. Donny holds on to her tightly and I like to think he knows he has his granddaughter with him. Maybe, it's a spastic movement on his part, but he certainly appears to enjoy their ride.

The other emotion he shows more frequently is crying. It usually happens when he hears familiar hymns or music and it always makes me cry too. I attended Christmas Eve services with him this past Christmas and he cried the whole half-hour of church. It makes me wonder how much is getting through to his brain. In a way I hope he has stopped thinking because it would be awful for him to be aware he's trapped in his body and can't do anything about it.

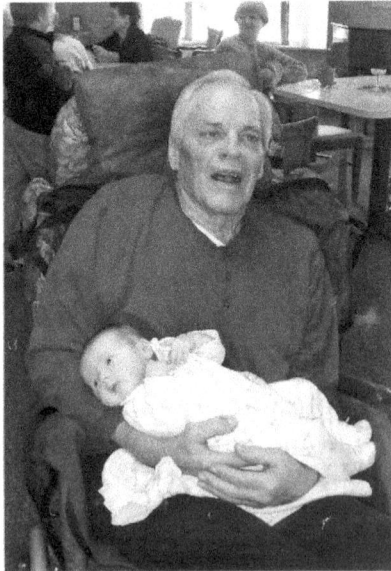

Donny with Granddaughter Lyla

Physically, he looks pretty good. He eats everything you put in his mouth and has no trouble chewing or swallowing. He's lost forty pounds in the two and a-half years, but it's a good weight for his frame and, he's maintained that same weight for several months. His pacemaker keeps ticking away and he could live like this for a long time. I've been told that many dementia patients outlive their caregivers and at this rate, it could happen for us.

Sharing

I started to go to a support group back in 2007 when we were having our tough times. I went faithfully for about two years, but found it was making me more depressed. I have been on antidepressants for a long time now and this group certainly didn't help. Several men there said that they visited their loved one every day, spending five to six hours a day with them. If you loved them, they said, that's what you have to do. It made me feel awful and I went home and cried all evening. I just couldn't do that and furthermore, I don't think it would do Donny one bit of good if I did come daily and spend hours there. Most of the time, he's not even aware of my presence. I think it's fine if that's what they want to do. Each situation is different. These men were quite old and, perhaps had nothing better to do. Although that may sound cynical, I think it's true. I certainly would be there if I felt I could do any good and if it would help Donny. What works best for me is to go there and feed him at noon when I can. It makes me feel useful and that I am helping him. I need to have a life away from the nursing home, yet still feel like I am there for him.

Many of my friends go south for the winter like we used to do when Donny was well. I feel envious of them, but there's no way I could go for a long period of time with him at the home. My day will come and if not, that's the way it's supposed to be. I have done some traveling and been gone for short periods of time. I feel fortunate that I can do that. I always go with an anxious knot in my stomach and my cell phone close at hand.

The last several months, I feel that I have found some good that I can do. About six people have come to me and asked for advice about how to handle their spouse who has some sort of dementia. Again, each case is different and I can tell them what I've learned from my experience. I've returned to the support group, for now and hope that I can help other people. I still have to deal with the people who say that if you love someone, you'll sit by their side every day for many hours.

In the fall of 2008, my daughter, her husband, Tom and their two beautiful little girls moved in with me "temporarily." Some people have told me that God works in mysterious ways and that is what He did to help me get through these tough times. We all frequently go to church with Donny at the home. My sons are supportive also, but distance and having busy families and jobs of their own prevent them from being a daily support, but I know that they are there when I need them.

Not as Golden as I Hoped

Sharon – December 2010

Our golden wedding anniversary was on the 17th of this month. It should have been a happy family time. Instead, I dreaded the day as it approached. My daughter had a housewarming/holiday party which was a masquerade for our anniversary. Unbeknownst to me, she had invited many of my friends with instructions not to mention the anniversary.

It was a very pleasant evening and it made me realize there are still many good things in life. Our lives are not what I envisioned years ago, but life does go on. I'd like to meet whoever said that retirement years should be our golden years. That is not true for many people. My advice is to enjoy every day, make good memories with your loved ones and don't wish your life away. Each day is a gift.

Society's Perspective

Mike – December 2010

Dementia Radar (Demdar)

Wikipedia defines Gaydar as "the intuitive ability to assess some-one's sexual orientation as gay, bisexual, or straight". I think all of us also possess Demdar (Dementia Radar). It's the intuitive ability to identify dementia behavior in other people. My guess is that Gaydar, Demdar and the ability to drive a car are all similar in that most everyone thinks they are pretty good at it. We all think we are way better than the average person.

Demdar may be left over from our evolution where people "culled the herd" of those that were not thinking clearly. Society might have killed off people who had diseased minds so that they would not reproduce and cause more problems. Back then, a dis-eased mind probably would not have been caused by dementia because people rarely got old enough to have that problem. But the symptoms would have been similar and maybe that's why we have Demdar today.

Gaydar is not inherently bad. Noticing that a person is gay can be like noticing they have blond hair or a nice figure. It may be none of your business, but it's just another fact about a person you've noticed.

Because we like to talk, we share the results of our Gaydar and our Demdar with our spouse and close friends. Once the intu-ition is confirmed, we switch to looking for behavior that supports our preconceived stereotypes. For example: "Did you notice how he couldn't remember his son's, wife's, father's name. He really is slipping."

This is not to say that being gay is a disease like dementia. But rather that people speculate on both and gossip about both.

I was making small talk today with a client while we waited for our meeting to start. She said, "Your office is off Kasota Avenue, is that fun bar still down the road?" At the end of the meeting we were talking about dropping something off and she asked where our office was. I reminded her it was on Kasota. She said, "Oh yeah, I knew that." My Demdar antenna picked that up and made a note. Next time I see her I will be paying a little closer attention to see if I can confirm my intuition.

Increased Sensitivity

Again, according to Wikipedia (so you know it's a fact) "*ABC News' 20/20* reported that Gaydar does exist but it may work better for gay people and those who pay attention to issues around sexual orientation because they have more invested interest in knowing if someone is gay."

I think the same thing applies to Demdar. Those who have spent a lot of time around people with dementia are usually better able to spot it.

Bring it on Themselves?

When I was young we went to a meeting in the basement of the church to hear two real live alcoholics tell about the disease. One lady said the first thing she thought about every morning when she got up was making sure she had something to drink that night. The other person told us about losing his family to alcohol. After a while one older person stood up and said, "Isn't an alcoholic just someone with no will power?"

I think that person was questioning whether alcoholism is a disease or a character flaw. I think the conventional wisdom says it's a disease. It may not be politically correct, but at some level I believe that a character flaw contributes to the situation and to blame it all on a disease is taking the easy way out.

In general we accept that behavior influences health. When told an acquaintance has lung cancer, the first question is, "Does he smoke?" The same thing happens with liver cancer or diabetes. We want to hold people accountable for their problems.

Susan Sontag, in *Illness as Metaphor*, writes about the phenomenon of blaming people for their illnesses:

"With the modern diseases (once TB, now cancer), the romantic idea that the disease expresses the character is invariably extended to assert that the character causes the disease—because it has not expressed itself. Passion moves inward, striking and blighting the deepest cellular recesses...Such preposterous and dangerous views manage to put the onus of the disease on the patient."

There are a number of books that give recommendations for keeping your brain healthy to avoid or prolong the onset of dementia. I recommend Dr. Amen's books. Some of their advice makes sense to everyone, such as eat right, don't drink too much and exercise your body. His books also talk about vitamins, red wine, blueberries (Dr. Amen calls them brainberries) and brain exercises that seem to make a difference.

My Dad did not do all the things recommended in these books. Even at the time I thought he should read, do crosswords, walk, exercise, stop watching TV and do things that might make his situation better. However, it's impossible and pointless to try to determine the amount he brought the disease on himself. None of us takes as good a care of ourselves as we should. None of us deserve dementia.

Does a Disease "fit" the Person?

I think people that know Dad feel sorry for him. However at some level they are not surprised by it either. Maybe it's because his Dad had Alzheimer's, or the fact that he has had the disease for a long time, or that he did not engage in mentally stimulating activities, but it just seems somehow appropriate that he has the disease.

I think it's human nature that we feel certain people "fit" with certain diseases. Even though smart people like Susan Sontag tell us we shouldn't "put the onus of the disease on the patient", we still do.

Many people hope to die in their sleep, or on the golf course, or in bed having sex, or something fun and exciting. The reality is that we don't get to choose. For most of us, some disease or ailment will choose us. I personally would like to die:

- Preventing terrorists from completing a suicide mission
- Saving a child from drowning
- As pharaoh and have a pyramid built for me

When I am winning at cards, I attribute it to my superior skill. When I lose, I attribute it to bad cards. I will probably have the same feeling about dementia. If dementia passes me by, it will be because of the great care I will have given my mind and body. If I get dementia, it will be bad genes.

Lowest Level Caste

Everyone has heard about the Hindu caste system in India. The lowest group is the untouchables. A person in a higher caste does not even want the shadow of an untouchable to cross over them. It sucks to be an untouchable.

I think people with brain disorders (including dementia) are the lowest caste in our society today. Kids call one another "retards" when they want to give a big insult. Or they might say they are going to the "funny farm."

At the other end of the spectrum of life, it's common to hear someone say with pride, "Mom finally died, but she was sharp as a tack right up until the end." To me that implies some accomplishment or a dignified state of being. As if Mom had looked at all the alternatives and decided to keep her mental facilities right up until her big exit.

Dementia is also a social stigma. As Eleanor Cooney said in *Death in Slow Motion*: "When I did introduce her to someone, she forgot that person instantly. A long, fun dinner party would evaporate from her memory overnight. What's the point of fun if you can't remember it? And the sad truth is that when people catch a whiff of dementia, they back off quickly. When the party's over, they don't call back. Who can blame them?"[i]

I was out with my Mom having lunch at a restaurant and a former school teacher, Mr. F was there having lunch. Mom told me that Mr. F was having mental issues and was requiring help. He was with another teacher friend of his who seemed to be taking care of him. Maybe I imagined it, but Mr. F had the look of someone not all there. I shook my head and looked at him with pity, forgetting that I hated when people talked about Dad that way. News about someone losing their mind travels very quickly.

Even within a long-term care facility the residents seem to have an awareness of every other resident's mental state. They talk amongst themselves and avoid the crazy people because when they talk, they don't make any sense. I heard one resident of the GRV say, "At least I'm not in the Rainbow Room."

I think this is very hard on a person with dementia. Through no fault of their own they have been relegated to the lowest caste in our society. It sucks to be an untouchable.

Spouse's Perspective

Sharon – December 2010

Social Adjustments

Donny and I always had a very active social life even though we both worked long hours and had four kids. We always had time for friends and doing fun things. Early on, our fun was playing cards while the kids played around us, or taking the family swimming and fishing. We tried camping, but that wasn't so great—we had a pouring rain that night and the tent flooded. That was the end of that.

Later, we got into golf, still played lots of cards and also liked to go dancing with friends. When our children were in high school, we attended many football, basketball and wrestling events. For several years, those were our extracurricular activities.

Donny was always friendly, fun to be around and liked by everyone. He was never a leader but a follower and a cheerful one at that. Everybody liked him and I can't remember him ever having any enemies. He worked hard and played hard. When he sold his bees and I quit my nursing job, we were able to spend several winters in Texas with a large group of golfing friends. I have such good memories of those winters.

As his mental condition started to deteriorate, the people who were close to him could see it, but many could not. People would imply that it was my imagination or my fault, but his condition gradually became more evident to everyone. I even had one friend who laughed at me like it was all one big joke, probably on me. That hurt.

After Donny was in the nursing home, my son Dean and I went out for dinner in a local establishment one evening. There was a group of three couples, there and I knew them all. One of the men was a prominent person in town. Talking with a slur, he hollered out for the whole world to hear, "Well, Dean, does your father know you anymore?" Dean kept his temper, but we were both very upset and embarrassed. People can be such jerks.

It's a Couple's World

A common expression you hear people saying is, "Where's your better half today," or "How is your better half?" Now I know what a 'half' person feels like and I'm really missing the other half. There's a big hole in my life.

A while back, I was visiting with a friend whose husband died not too long ago. She was telling me how hard it was to be living alone and making decisions by herself. Although he had been sick a long time, her husband was alert until he died and I'm sure it has been a big adjustment. My adjustment has been much more gradual, but I don't think any easier. I've been making "our decisions" alone for a long time, but I still have a husband. Widows have their time of grieving and for the most part, can get on with their lives. But I'm sure they always have that hole as well. My grieving and that of my family began many years ago and is ongoing, but yet I have to get on with my life also. Widows can start a new, single life, but I feel like I am limbo—I'm not really a free person. I'm involved in activities that keep me busy, but my life has certainly changed.

One day, I was discussing with that same friend, where we fit now and what our reason for being on this earth was. I've thought about that many times since. Other than being with my family, I feel most comfortable at the nursing home when I am feeding Donny. It feels like I belong there, but I can't sit there for hours since there's no communication between us. I visit with many of the other lonesome people and maybe that's my purpose in life now. I wish I knew. I do feel better when I'm helping others or listening to their problems. There are a lot of needy people in the world.

Still, truly it's a couple's world and I know that's a cliché, but living it's understanding it. Many of our couple friends will ask about Donny. They're friendly when I see them, but, generally speaking, I am not included in the "couples" events. I've seen this happen with other widows, so I don't think I'm being paranoid about it. I try not to take it personally. That's just the way it's.

Last summer, I spent an afternoon with some college friends and among them were a widow and a divorcee. They started talking about the men they had met through on-line dating. Some were good experiences and some not so good and we were all having a good laugh. One of them said to me, "Sharon, you should try it. Maybe you could have some fun." I just looked at her and said that I wasn't free to do that. Again, I felt like I was in limbo.

The problem is that it's hard for me to just have fun, to laugh and just relax. It's not possible to completely forget the deep sadness in me. I am very thankful for my family and my friends who are supportive and provide me with some good times. It's just not the way I envisioned my retirement years to be. My other half is here but not here.

Downsize Again

Now I would like to sell my house and move to a low maintenance town house which would be much easier for me. My retirement dream home is a dream home no more. It isn't going to be easy, but I know it's something I have to do. Last summer was rainy which meant lots of lawn mowing. We have a huge lawn and there was a lot of outside work to be done too. My knee started bothering me, which eventually needed some minor surgery and I felt worn out. I decided God was trying to tell me something, so I made the decision to put my house up for sale. My granddaughter told me that she will be very sad when I move and I said, "I know."

Many people are going through similar experiences and I'm sure many people have it much worse. But going through them with a spouse in a nursing home adds another twist. It makes it even more difficult when the spouse has dementia and can't communicate. I just hope I can feel like a whole person again someday. Does time really cure all of these things? I hope I live that long.

Comfort Measures Only

About two months after Donny went to the retirement home, he fell out of the wheelchair one evening and the nurse told me he couldn't move his shoulder. They had called the ambulance and he was on the way to the hospital. Nothing was broken and the ambulance brought him back to the GRV. That shoulder had been immovable for a long time due to severe arthritis. If they had called me first, I would have nixed the ambulance trip. After that, I asked GRV to notify me before any trip to the clinic or hospital.

A couple of weeks later I received a telephone call from the GRV saying that Donny had a high fever. They were wondering if they should call the doctor or bring him to the hospital. I suggested that they try Tylenol and see how he was in the morning. Late that same evening, I received another call from a frantic, concerned nurse saying that his fever was still quite high and he really needed antibiotics. She kept trying to get me to consent and I finally relented and gave her permission to give him some antibiotics. I felt really guilty because first of all, I was out of town and could not go right to the GRV, and second because I hadn't agreed to the antibiotics in the afternoon. His fever resolved in a few days.

Donny's normal doctor was not on call that weekend and the doctor on call was unfamiliar with Donny. When I got home later that week I spoke to Donny's normal doctor and I told him about what had happened. He just shook his head and told me not to let that happen again, that pneumonia would be Donny's best friend. I was taken aback by that, but after giving it some thought, I came to the same conclusion. I have done some research on Pick's disease and read that at the end, victims have trouble swallowing and can choke to death. Because he has a pacemaker it's unlikely his heart will be the cause of his death. The pacemaker already had pulled him through a lengthy grand mal seizure at the Litchfield center when the doctor did not think he would ever regain consciousness. So given the options, pneumonia would be a friend.

Our doctor told me it was perfectly acceptable–that he supported my decision to leave a "comfort measure only" on his chart. That would mean there would be no clinic visits or hospital stays, no antibiotics or life prolonging procedures or medicines. The doctor would still see him on a regular basis at the GRV, so it's not like he would be neglected.

Coming from a nursing background, I have always believed in treating diseases aggressively, restoring and prolonging life when possible. In general, life was good and death was bad.

However, I also worked extensively with our local hospice program and learned that death can be met with dignity by being comfortable and surrounded by loving people. I remember many instances when death was a welcome release for a person who was terminally ill and had been for a long time. Although it's still a time of sadness, there's a feeling of relief for the person who's been ill for a long time.

More and more literature is coming out about people being able to make their own choices about their medical care and making their own living wills expressing their feelings about end-of-life decisions. People can refuse extensive testing and procedures if there is no chance of improvement.

Recently, a friend of mine with a very ill husband was telling me how they were both wearing out travelling to out-of- town doctors and enduring the many tests that doctors want to do. When asked if she felt these tests were necessary, her reply was no. The tests repeated everything that had already been done and nothing had helped. I reminded her that she had the option to refuse the tests. She could let her husband's care be managed by their local family doctor. She thought that was a good idea and said she would think about it.

Guilt often enters the picture as people feel they have to do what the doctor orders. Doctors are great and we need to depend on their advice, but their duty in medicine is to cure and prolong life. There comes a time when we have to think of what is best for the patient. The same logic holds true for all terminally ill patients. Fight as long as you can, but when the time comes, check out all of the options and make the best decision you can for yourself and your loved one.

At the time I'm writing this, Donny has been imprisoned in his body for almost four years. He cannot walk or talk or feed himself. It's questionable if he knows any of his family members, although occasionally he does show some emotion. At first, we got an occasional smile when he saw us, but it's been a long time since we've seen that. Now, he sobs and cries during church services, or sometimes when a family member visits. His crying breaks my heart.

Donny is receiving good care. He appears to be at peace–at least most of the time. We have put him in God's hands and let His will be done. In the meantime, we'll continue to be there when we can and continue to be his advocate for comfort measures only.

I did not make the "comfort measures only" decision lightly. I also understand that some people will disagree with me. However, as a nurse and the wife of a person suffering from a terminal illness, I have come to believe that "comfort measures only" makes sense in many situations.

Demand of God

In the fall after "the worst year", the year he threatened me and was then hospitalized, I was fortunate to travel to Israel with a church group. I was very anxious about leaving Donny for ten days, but I'd arranged to rent a phone once I got there that would allow me to receive or send calls from home. Due to poor communication at our first hotel and a language barrier, I never got the phone. I was very upset. I found out later that the phone was at that hotel, but the people working either didn't know about it or didn't understand us. I ended up having to pay for it anyway, but got credit for a free phone for my next trip to Israel, which will never happen.

My emotions were still pretty raw and I was willing to tell the story of my awful summer to anybody who would listen to me. One day I was telling a woman that I prayed every day for my children and grandchildren not to get the disease. She was a strong believer in prayer and she told me, "Don't ask God to protect them, demand it. Tell him it's unacceptable for your children and grandchildren to get dementia. It worked for me when I demanded help for a relative."

I didn't know how to respond to this advice then and I still don't know if it appropriate to demand anything from God. I have always believed in putting problems into God's hands and letting Him deal with it. I tried "demanding" for a while, but it didn't seem right to me. Prayer is definitely important and underused and how you do is up to each person.

Son's Perspective

Do I have Dementia?

The Alzheimer's Association website (www.alz.org) devotes a lot of space toward helping people distinguish between normal aging versus Alzheimer's symptoms. So it must be a common concern shared by a lot of people. As I read through the lists, it seems that the distinction is largely a matter of degree. For example, forgetting an appointment is normal, but forgetting it was ever scheduled is more of a red flag.

Reluctant Acceptance

"We sat in silence for a while. Finally he smiled ruefully and said, 'Doggone, I never thought I'd lose my mind.' There was an unspoken clause implicit at the start of this sentence—I've tried to think of all the ways I might get old, but—and I heard it at least as clearly as I heard the part he spoke. I understood, abruptly, that he had wondered how they would come to him, old age and death and now he was even a little bemused that they should take this unexpected form as they approached."[ii]

James Nichols, the person in the above quote, was a fourth generation minister, a retired professor from Princeton Theological Seminary. It's ironic that someone with so much education and that had made their living with their mind succumbed to the disease. There are many examples of highly educated and successful people who have dementia.

Somewhat Oblivious

Maybe it was because Dad had frontal lobe dementia, but we rarely ever used the term "Alzheimer's" with Dad. Alzheimer's seemed like a much worse word to him. Maybe it was because that was the disease Grandpa had. I remember riding in Dad's pickup and he asked why he couldn't drive anymore. I said it was "the dementia thing." He said, "Dementia thing, I don't know about that." I don't think he ever accepted that he had a disease.

I think he felt that the world had taken a wrong turn somewhere but his mind was okay. It's like the episode from The Twilight Zone where the world shifted and everyone started using different words. To the man in the show, his mind was still okay, but the world was losing it. I think that episode is very similar to the way Dad felt.

Maybe part of it was that Dad was never very self-aware. Or maybe it was part of his coping or hiding mechanism. But he said very little to indicate he was aware of the disease.

Self-Awareness Test

Somebody told me you can distinguish someone with the disease because they won't realize they are losing their mind. It's like unforgivable sin, if you worry you have committed it, then you haven't. If you worry you have dementia, then that is an indicator that you don't. I don't think it's a good test because there are enough stories in the literature about people like James Nichols who, at least in the early stages, know that something is going off track.

Do I want to Know?

I have heard there are DNA tests that can be a good indicator of dementia. However, it's the old question; if there is no known treatment, would you want to know? If I knew the test would come back negative, then I'd want them done so I could quit worrying about it. But if it came back positive, it would be very difficult to go through life knowing what was ahead of me.

I can't explain why I won't do the DNA tests but have done other self-tests. Probably part of it's the confidentiality question. I would not even want my wife to know if it was positive. Part of it's probably the imprecise nature. I already know there is dementia in my family history; I don't need another "good indicator" which wouldn't be conclusive anyway.

Descendant's Worry

I think it's common for a person with a history of the disease in their family to worry about it. For example: "It's my turn to think of it—of death—and I do. I wonder how it will come to me. Unlike Dad, though—but largely because of him—I think often of the possibility that I may lose my mind."[iii]

With my family history, I worry all the time that I will be the next in line. It's the first thing that enters my mind whenever I forget any little fact. I also worry that most everybody who knows me well will be paying close attention to my behavior to see if I exhibit any symptoms of the disease. Their Demdar antennae will be on high-alert when talking with me. Maybe I am just being paranoid, but because everyone tells me I look and act just like Dad, it's hard to believe they would not also look for the trait that defined the last years of his life.

Several times when I have told people that my Dad is suffering from this disease, they have said, "Do you know it can be hereditary?" I always say, "Yep, I've heard that." I always thought that was like asking the slightly overweight woman if she was pregnant; nothing good ever comes from that question.

I absolutely hate the idea of anyone looking at me like I looked at my Dad.

I know I can't stop people from scrutinizing me. The more I protest, the more I would be scrutinized. This sensitivity is my issue and the best thing I can do is to not make it an issue. I have reviewed all the lists and taken the self-tests and none of them indicate I have the disease. I am doing what I can to stay healthy. I just need to let things take their course and hope for the best.

The other thing I do, of course, is pray. I pray most every day that dementia will skip me, my kids, my siblings and their kids. I hope God will give our family a break from this disease for a while.

Money and Moral Dilemmas

Mike – December 2010

Long-Term Care Insurance

We were fortunate to have long-term care insurance. I'm not sure the new policies are as generous or very easy to get. I worked on a project unrelated to Dad helping insurance companies that sell long-term care policies. The insurance companies use both questionnaires and client screenings to look for any sign of dementia. They don't want to sell a policy to someone like Dad who will require very expensive care for many years. My impression is that if you have any history of dementia in your family, you'll have a hard time finding a policy and if you do find one, it will be very expensive.

Who Should Pay?

Around the time Dad was diagnosed, we went to an attorney to get his affairs in order. The attorney said that a couple of years before he would have recommended putting all Dad and Mom's assets into a trust. But they've closed the loopholes on trusts, so he recommended that Dad gift them to one or more of his kids. There's a five-year look- back period, but after five years, the nursing home has no claim on the assets.

So that's what we did. I have heard many families do the same kind of thing. They do not want the assets of the family going to the nursing home.

The average price for long-term care in the United States is $200 per day. GRV is less expensive at only $150 per day. The price has increased four times in the last twelve months and I would bet the price keeps on increasing. Dad has been at GRV three and a-half years so far and could easily be there another seven. If my Dad ends up staying at the GRV for ten years, it will cost $547,500. The long-term care policy pays $112 per day, so that really helps our situation. Even so, my family's contribution is significant. Some assets have been sold to keep the bills paid.

We still have a couple years to go on the five year look back. After that, we should be able to have Medicaid pay for the portion of Dad's care not covered by long-term care insurance. Therefore, we think our family will be successful in shielding most of its assets from the big bad retirement home.

Condemned to Poverty

I'm not sure if it's fair for us to expect Medicaid to pay for Dad's care. But I am also not sure if it's fair to expect Mom to pay either. She would like to go south in the winter with her friends. She would like to travel with her grandkids. She's only seventy and her Dad was active into his nineties. The disease has already put her through hell. Should it also condemn her to poverty for the rest of her life?

One friend told me that his Dad was in the nursing home for a short rehabilitative stay after surgery. His Dad was paying full-price for his care. This friend knew many of the other people in the home. He said it irked him that "Old Mr. S, who never worked a day in his life, gets the same care as my Dad." It's very easy to feel like a chump for paying full price when it seems like so many don't pay at all.

I can get excited about saving for the future when it's something I'm looking forward to. I've saved for my kid's education, my retirement and my cabin. But it's really hard to get excited about saving for a nursing home. I tell myself it's my duty and I have a moral obligation to take care of myself, even if it means a nursing home. But saving for a nursing home is way down on my list.

I know some people purchase long-term care insurance and I applaud them. However, in an age when most people haven't even saved enough for retirement, I doubt many have the assets necessary to fund their own long-term care.

"Medicare covers about 12% of private nursing home costs while Medicaid covers about 50%. The Veteran's Administration nursing home operations bring total government support of nursing home costs to about 70% of the total. Such a large reliance on government support has made nursing homes vulnerable to vagaries in state and Federal reimbursement policies towards nursing homes.[iv]"

It seems ingrained in people that, one way or another, the government will pay. They may complain about the "entitlement mentality" of other people in other social programs, but they view long-term care differently. The conventional wisdom seems to be that it's prudent financial planning to make sure your assets don't get used for long-term care.

I don't think people's attitudes will change. Most people hate the idea of being put into a nursing home. The last thing they want to do is save money to be put there. But many of us will require long-term care. According to the *Minneapolis Star Tribune*, "a person has a 70% chance of needing some type of long-term care after age 65, costing an average of $48,000. For about 6% of those people, costs will exceed $100,000."[v]

The other factor is that dementia usually sets in after several years of retirement. So the person's retirement nest egg has already been somewhat depleted. Also, dementia does not fall on a person all at once. They probably have their suspicions and will spend or gift as much money as they can. You might as well live it up if you suspect the worst.

However, I think the best solution is to find a cure for dementia because dementia is the underlying reason so many people require long-term care.

What is "Best Care"?

In my experience, a person with dementia craves the constant companionship of close family members. It's well put in the following quote: "I understand that there is only one drug in the world that can keep my mother calm and centered and I am that drug."[vi] Without that "drug," the patient will act out.

It's not physically possible for one person to provide care all by themselves for any length of time. I estimate it would have taken three or four full-time equivalents (FTEs) to provide the kind of care my Dad would have preferred. Ideally all the FTEs would have been close family members.

I think my Dad would have preferred to stay on the farm and have his wife and kids wander around the sheds helping him organize stuff. We would have planted trees and helped him collect scrap metal. Because we provided him companionship and supervision, he could have lived out his life much like a young boy. Given the circumstances, it would have been the best possible quality of life.

In that world, Mom and we kids would have provided the care. As a family, we would have been the drug he needed and his acting-out would have been minimized. It would, however, have meant putting the lives of at least three other people on hold.

We were not willing to make that sacrifice. We told ourselves we were looking at the bigger picture. In college, I learned that one of the principles of John Stuart Mill's utilitarian thinking was producing the greatest amount of good for the greatest number of people. Measuring "good" is tough. In our case, we concluded that even if Dad had asked to stay on the farm and have us around, it was not in the best interests of the total family to do that.

The other factor was that we made an assumption about what Dad would have thought before dementia, not what he thought after the onset of dementia. Dad always wanted the best for his wife and kids; there is no way he would have wanted us to put our lives on hold for an extended period of time for him.

The point is that the concept of "best care" is not as straight forward as it appears.

The Right Thing

Reading the last couple pages, it's hard not to feel guilty. My family is not willing to take care of Dad ourselves. Nor are we willing to pay someone else for the full cost of his care. I will only say that we visit him more often than most patients get visited. And we are trying to do the best we can. Please don't judge us unless you have lived through this nightmare.

Taboo Subjects

Mike – December 2010

Enabling Behavior

It's common that alcoholics have spouses who are enablers. Partners who cover up for alcoholics behavior during the time they are intoxicated and after. It's generally assumed that this enabling behavior allows alcoholics to persist in their condition longer than they otherwise might. In fact, enabling behavior is bad because it delays alcoholics from hitting bottom. That is the only way they might agree to get treatment.

Enabling behavior is also common with dementia. The spouse or the entire family tries their best to hide the disease from the outside world. They make excuses for the person, withdraw from social engagements and start spending more time alone.

Dementia and alcoholism are also similar in that once you've been accused of having the disease, it's virtually impossible to change the world's mind. You are guilty for the rest of your life. The difference, of course, is that an alcoholic can get treatment and become a recovering alcoholic. There are no recovering dementia patients.

In my opinion, enabling behavior when there is dementia is not necessarily bad for the following reasons. First, because the knowledge of dementia so changes the way the world interacts with the person, you are better off hiding it as long as possible. Second, the person with dementia doesn't really have a choice. Assuming that person is getting all the professional care possible,

117

there is no a reason to tell the rest of the world. Finally, hiding the disease will make the progression of the disease as slow as possible.

Sex

Several books on dementia indicate that people with the disease still want physical stimulation including massaging the person's head and face. I think they may be wanting more than that. Here is an excerpt from Eleanor Cooney's book.

"Tricia at Sheffield House would like to talk to you," he says and hands me the phone. Oh, God. Tricias's the nurse. What is it? Is Mom just running low on underwear, or has she hit somebody in the face? Broken someone's nose? I'm sorry to have to tell you this...

"Eleanor?" says Tricia, "I'm calling about your mother."

"Lay it on me," I say.

"There's been an incident," Tricia begins carefully, "that I'm obligated to tell you about." I brace myself. "Um—your mother was discovered this morning asleep in a male resident's bed. She wasn't wearing anything except a shirt... " I laugh out loud in relief...

"God!" I say. "That's GREAT!"[vii]

This story is not unique. A nurse that works at a retirement home said that many people with dementia are interested in sex. They are required to notify the family and sometimes they have a hard time with that, especially if the other spouse is still alive. They don't want Mom getting action in the long-term care facility while Dad is still living alone at home. Sometimes drugs are used to curtail this behavior.

Mom told me that when she was working as a nurse at the hospital, it was fairly common that old men would try to touch her boobs. The nurses discussed it among themselves and knew who to watch out for.

I don't know if this is good or bad or just human nature. Based on my observation, a person's mind may be leaving them, but they hang on to the human physical needs like touch and sex.

Legacy

From time to time, all of us consider how we will be remembered. One of the most common things we hope for is to be remembered as good loving parents. But beyond that, what will we be remembered for and for how long will that memory last?

On both sides of my family, enterprising people have done a lot of work on our family tree. Once we had a family reunion and our relatives who still live in Norway attended. There were huge printouts showing the family trees, which looked more like spider webs because they were not going up or down to one person. What the spider web showed for each person was basic: name, date of birth, date of death and for those that were on one side or the other of immigration to the United States, a place of residence.

There was very little detail about any of the people beyond the family tree. For one couple, there was a story about the eight brothers who all set up farms next to one another. Another story was about a man who hardly ever left the farm because he was working so hard (this could be said about most of them) and that he met his wife when she was riding on her father's wagon to bring milk to the creamery. I'm sure there is a rich life behind every one of those names. But I don't have a burning desire to research their lives or hear their stories. In fact I have seen several families dispose of old family pictures. Many times they did not even know who was in the pictures.

I think most of us will be pretty much forgotten in two generations. We remember our grandparents, but usually not any farther back. I have a foggy recollection of my great grandma because she used to play hide-and- seek with us kids despite the fact that she was pretty old. Maybe it would be different if you had someone famous in your family tree. But my impression of those families is that they are just trying to hold onto faded glory. Maybe that is just sour grapes on my part.

Even if I experience huge success in business and pass a fortune onto my kids, my legacy will probably not be remembered much longer than two generations. Everyone has heard the conventional wisdom about a fortune in a family. Generation One sacrifices and risks everything. This generation works hard, benefits from good luck and creates a huge company. Generation Two is not afraid to enjoy the finer things in life, but they work hard to keep the company going. By the time Generation Three rolls around, the company is not doing as well and they squander what is left.

Maybe being wildly successful in something means you will be remembered for another generation or two, but probably not much more. And almost certainly not remembered by anyone outside of your family.

I think Dad will be remembered for three things. One, that he had an unusual occupation, a beekeeper. Two, that he planted thousands of trees. Three, that he died of dementia.

It stinks to think that dementia has to be part of his legacy. But the good thing is–if you can call it a good thing– is that Dad will only be remembered for two or three generations. After that, it will be lost.

"All men are like grass and all their glory is like the flowers of the field. The grass withers and the flowers fall."[viii] In other words, don't take yourself too seriously, because we are here only for a short while.

Or, as a beekeeper might say, "Even a strong hive won't last forever."

Violence then Drugs

Mike

Dad told me that he had never been in a fight in his life. The closest he came was in high school when an older kid threatened him. Dad said he pushed him against a locker and that was the end of it.

When I was older, a friend of my Dad's told me Dad was one of those men that other men didn't mess with. Even as he got older, he had a look that if pushed, he could hold his own.

Most times when you hear about violence occurring in the context of dementia, a quote from the family will say something like, "That is not my Dad; it's the disease acting out. Dad doesn't have a violent bone in his body."

The Real Person

As Dad's disease progressed, certain behaviors became more pronounced. Some of the behaviors were good and some were bad. I found myself hoping that the good behaviors were Dad's true character coming through. Conversely, I blamed his bad behavior on the disease.

For example, Dad always had a sweet tooth. As the disease progressed, he ate more cookies and ice cream and other sweet things. We laughed about it and thought it was funny that he found enjoyment in sweets. That was an example of his good point endearing him to us during his decline.

On the other side, Dad was never very patient. When we were growing up he would want us outside working at a certain time. One day, I was sleeping late and Dad threw a glass of water in my face. Another time, when my brothers and I questioned one of his assignments, his response was, "If I tell you to stack babies in the corner, you should just do it." This impatience and dislike of being questioned also became more pronounced as the disease progressed. Needless to say, that behavior did not endear him to us.

My opinion is that dementia lays bare the real person. I think it's similar to the way alcohol affects some people. Sober, they would never say or do certain things, but drunk, they lose their inhibitions and say whatever is on their mind. Before dementia, they would never act out with inappropriate behavior, but as the disease progresses, they become less able to control themselves.

I think that, at some level, Dad was fighting the disease every step of the way. Or maybe he was fighting the way the world reacted to him because of the disease. He hated being unable to keep up with the conversation, being the subject of other conversations and being treated like a child. He worked hard to try to hide the disease and keep things be as normal as they could be.

As the disease progressed, he fought back using every tool he had, including physical violence. He was probably torn up inside. For example, he knew he should not poop in bed, but hated being told not to do it. It was not that he was mad at Mom for telling him, he was mad at the situation. Mom was just there.

However, this does not make violence acceptable. I am just trying to understand what would drive a person to that point. Violence is not limited to men. Many women with dementia also hit and kick and knock over things. They are just so mad and nobody seems to be listening to them. So they resort to the only tool they have which seems to get peoples undivided attention.

Resorting to violence is another example of how people with dementia revert back to infantile behavior.

Drugs

It seemed Dad went back and forth on a drug teeter-totter. He would have some condition or behavior like high blood pressure, knee surgery, violence, or a seizure. So they would give him some drugs, which would cause him to be a zombie. Then he would be taken off the drugs until some other unacceptable behavior happened.

Nursing homes are often accused of over-medicating patients to make them easier to care for. In our situation, I am not sure the home in Cosmos would have taken Dad if they had known Mom was not going to let him be heavily medicated.

The other thing that comes through in the literature is that many people with dementia are more sensitive to drugs. The dosages and typical mixes of drugs don't work, or work too much on people with dementia.

In society, drugs beget violence. In dementia, violence begets drugs.

Go Out the Way You Came In

When babies come into this world they need to be fed, have their diaper changed and be carried around everywhere. Many times, people with dementia become like that. Dad needed to be fed and have his diaper changed. He was in a wheel chair and was lifted from there to his bath and his bed. Whereas babies are moving in one direction, people with dementia are moving in the other.

In a way, a ward of dementia patients is similar to a preschool. You have a range of care needs and the staff needs to adjust their services for each patient. Sometimes when they get mad, they act out, sometimes violently. Toddlers get time outs and dementia patients get drugs. The most infantile don't respond well to games or having conversations with others. When they do talk, they want their Mommy or they want to go home.

Exiting this World

Sharon – March 15, 2011

On Wednesday morning, February 23, I received a call that Donny had thrown up after breakfast. He had eaten a huge meal and the nurse speculated he probably eaten too much, or maybe he had a flu bug. It didn't seem to be a huge concern–a bit unusual, but those things happen. I fed him his noon meal and he didn't do his normal, clean-the-plate thing; he drank some liquids and had some soda crackers. Later in the afternoon, I gave him some more liquids, some applesauce and more crackers. The nurses told me his vital signs were normal, so again, it was not a big concern.

Thursday morning, I received another call that he'd vomited a large amount of coffee ground emesis. When it appears like coffee grounds, it means it's partially digested blood and the bleeding is probably coming from the stomach. This was a life threatening concern. From that point on, it was all downhill for Donny.

By evening, his temperature and pulse had started to go up, both ominous signs. His abdomen was slightly distended and his respirations were more rapid. Mike and Sara were there with me. Donny was given a Tylenol suppository for his temperature and to relieve some of his symptoms. We all needed some sleep and because we knew Friday would be a long day, we left at 1 a.m. I wasn't sure he would live through the night, but I was only five minutes away if the home called me.

Soon after I arrived in the early morning, I knew this was the day he would die. He didn't have any more emesis, but he occasionally spit up dark liquid. He was not given anything orally, his breathing was getting more labored and his temp was up again.

125

These were comfort measures only, but he didn't appear conscious enough to experience pain.

Mike didn't totally accept what was happening. He said, "Maybe he will wake up and be better." He left to go do something. My third child was with us by that time and we took turns holding his hand and talking to him. About 1:00 p.m., his breathing became shallower and his abdomen more distended, probably from more bleeding. We could see his extremities getting blue, his respirations changed and at 2:00 p.m., he took his last breath. It was very peaceful.

When he actually died, I felt a profound sense of peace come over me. This past Sunday, I'd heard a sermon about having mountain moments–times when you know God is present. Donny's death was a mountain moment for me. We had all said our goodbyes and he too, was at peace at last.

Dad's Death

Mike

Dad's death was more of a relief for me than anything else. It sometimes seemed that tough old bird might live another 20 years. I regret that I was not there when he died. I was plowing snow out of my driveway. Maybe that's what Dad would have wanted anyway. Shouldn't be standing around when there is work to be done.

Donald S. Larson, 74

Donald Stanley Larson was born on June 17, 1936 on his parents' farm (David and Sylvia Larson) near Terrace Minnesota. He attended country school for eight years where he had to walk up hill both ways. He graduated in 1965 from Glenwood High School where he excelled in wrestling and track.

He farmed with his Dad, then a variety of jobs including construction, auto mechanic and manufacturing; until he figured out he should be a beekeeper in 1964. He was a beekeeper until he retired in 1995.

Donny met Sharon Gandrud at a Luther League party at the parsonage. On December 17, 1960, they were married at Barsness Lutheran Church. They lived on a farm by Terrace until they moved near Glenwood in 2003. Donny was a lifelong member of Chippewa Falls Lutheran Church where he was baptized, confirmed and now buried.

Donny loved being outside. He loved hunting, trapping, fishing and just walking in the woods. Over the years he planted thousands of trees. He knew the names of all the trees and birds and loved to teach them to his grandchildren. (Not that he named every tree and bird, but that he knew the species of the each.)

He took up golf when he was in his 40's. For a number of years he practiced or played almost every day. There was nothing half way about Don. He will also be remembered for his dancing. "Crazy legs Larson" really lived the adage "dance like no one's watching."

Donny died at the Glenwood Retirement Village on Friday February 25, 2011. He suffered from frontal lobe dementia and died of complications. The disease which took so much away from the last years of his life at least let him die peacefully, surrounded by family.

Donny is survived by his wife Sharon, four children Michael (Karen) of Bloomington, MN, Paul of Oak Ridge, NJ, Dean (Mimi) of Burnsville, MN and Sara (Tom) Stadtherr of Glenwood, MN. He has ten granddaughters. Natasha, Alexis, Rebecca, Melissa, Julia, Mary, Anna, Sylvia, (all Larsons) Soffia and Lyla Stadtherr. Also surviving is a sister Carol (Odell) Anderson of Onalaska, WI, nieces, nephews and many cousins.

Preceding him in death were his parents and a niece, Nancy Anderson.

Memorial donations, unless otherwise designated, will be split between the Glenwood Retirement Village, Chippewa Falls Lutheran Church and the Alzheimer's Association.

Eulogy for Dad

Mike – March 1, 2011

For the last several years I have prayed that God take Dad sooner rather than later. So today is a good day. I believe Dad has gone to heaven and is in a better place.

I think this disease started impacting my Dad twenty years ago. So it was a part of him for about one fourth of his life. However, it was not his entire life.

I remember the time when I was in high school and we were coming home from a hunting trip and we got into a deep conversation. This hardly ever happened with Dad, but it did then. He told me what I should look for in a wife. He said, "I was lucky, I found a wife who is pretty and has a good personality." Thank you God for letting him have fifty years with Mom.

Five years ago I took Dad and Grandma for a drive in the car. Dad was still living at home but he was obviously not himself. On this day I could tell something was bothering him. Finally he said something about heaven. I asked him if he believed Jesus was God's son. He said, "Yes, absolutely". Then I told him that as I understood it, he was going to heaven. That seemed to put his mind at ease. God, please welcome him.

Last night at the visitation several people came up to me and told me I look just like my Dad. Sometimes I am embarrassed by that. I don't want people to see my Dad in me because that means I might have the disease. However, nobody knows what the future will bring. I have no reason to be embarrassed. Thank you God for letting him be my father.

I have shared the story of my last hunting trip with my Dad with a lot of you. There were many other "lasts" after that. His last time driving a car. The last time he hugged my Mom. The last time he called me Mike. You usually don't know it's a "last" when it happens. It's only later you realize it will never occur again.

God help me to appreciate every day like it's the last.

Advice for the Family

Mike – December 2010

The journey upon which you are embarking will not be fun. In fact it will be worse than you expect. Don't make the situation worse by feeling sorry for yourself but soldier through it as best you can. You didn't sign up for this but you need to deal with it. It's the right thing to do.

Dementia Umbrella

Sometimes Dementia and Alzheimer's are used interchangeable. But actually Alzheimer's is a subset of Dementia and it breaks down as follows:

60% Alzheimer's

20% Vascular dementia

10% Combination of Alzheimer's and Vascular dementia

10% Frontal lobe dementia or Pick's disease

In my experience, people with Alzheimer's are a little easier to deal with than people with Frontal Lobe Dementia. People with Alzheimer's seem more upbeat and quick to laugh off their situation. They repeat themselves more often and they have bad short-term memory.

People with Frontal Lobe Dementia are more ornery. They are frustrated with themselves and try to show the world they are still okay. Their short-term memory is not so bad and they seem to know what is going on. However, their behavior is bizarre. Whereas a person with Alzheimer's may wander off and get lost, a person with Frontal Lobe is more likely to run away on purpose.

Uncertainty of Diagnosis

First someone told us that they thought Dad had Alzheimer's. Then a test came back saying that he did not. Then we found out about the small strokes. We still don't know if they were a cause or effect of the disease. Finally a doctor gave us a diagnosis of Frontal Lobe Dementia. Even that, however, was probably subject to debate. There could have been some Alzheimer's thrown in there as well.

My impression is that pinpointing the exact disease is very difficult and probably not that important anyway. The behaviors are a little different, but the prognosis is the same. The disease will continue to progress. They will not go back to the way they were. Their best days are behind them and you have to deal with it.

Your loved one will have some good days but don't get your hopes up. Most likely they still have the disease. Enjoy the good times but don't pin your hopes on a cure. You will try to get new lifestyle patterns and do things to try to keep an even keel. But sooner or later another episode will happen which will leave you frustrated and disappointed. You will want to blame the person.

Uncertainty of Timing

Eventually we accepted that Dad had a disease. Then we spent lots of time wondering where Dad was in its progression. When should we tell people? When should we ask for outside help? How long should we keep Dad at home? There is a lot of second guessing and wondering if we should be stronger and better care givers. That if only we could hold out through the immediate crisis, things would settle down. Maybe Dad would even start to get better. All these thoughts go through your mind and make decisions very difficult.

Flying Blind

There is a huge amount of resources to draw upon. The Alzheimer's Association has a website that is packed with great information. Most towns have an Alzheimer's support group for the people themselves as well as their families. There are programs to have people come into your home and provide services. Despite all that, there were times we felt like we were flying blind. Dad's situation did not neatly fit into the patterns and there was no one that could give us definitive answers.

Betrayal

Several writers have mentioned their sense of betrayal in dealing with their loved one. It's one of the things that make the disease so cruel. You will be forced to make hard decisions over and over, with small things and big things. At some point you will look into the person's eyes and feel like you have betrayed them. I know I did.

Guilt

There are many layers of guilt in dealing with a person who has dementia. The big step of putting him into a nursing home was an obvious one. But there are little things all along the way. Is it ok to laugh at their mistakes? Can we ask a friend to take him for an afternoon? Should we have company over when we know he finds that stressful? How often should I visit him in the nursing home? Should I keep him in my thoughts? Why do people keep asking me about him when I am trying to get on with my life?

Spacey by Association

Some writers have said that caring for their loved one caused them to feel like they are losing their mind. I know my Mom felt that way at times. It's almost like you are pulled into their world so much that you start to think like them. I think this is just a temporary situation that goes away when you stop being the primary care provider but it's another phenomenon that makes the disease difficult to get through.

Worry

If you are a blood relative of the person with the disease, it would be weird if you didn't worry about having dementia yourself. Don't let it consume you. Don't obsess about it. Take care of yourself and pray a lot.

Drug Maze

You will probably be pulled into the great drug maze. You will learn about different kinds of drugs and research them on the internet, often times after they have already been administered to your loved one. You will hear reports about breakthroughs and experimental drugs and will be frustrated that your loved one is not getting something that fixes the problem.

At some point, you will probably want a drug to knock them out. This will probably occur when you are the primary care provider and your loved one is getting close to being physically or verbally abusive. Later, when you are not the primary care giver, you will complain they are overmedicated and demand it be stopped. Yet you will not see any hypocrisy in that action.

In my unscientific opinion, I think the fewer the drugs the better. However, accept the fact that during the disease's progression, drugs may be necessary and they may be a zombie for a short period of time. In my mind that's better than a strait jacket. Once they get through that phase the drugs will be unnecessary.

What Will People Think

What I worried about evolved over time. In the beginning I was embarrassed by Dad's behavior. Then I worried that people would take advantage of him. Further down the road I worried more about what people thought of how our family was dealing with the situation. And finally I spend time worrying that people see the disease in me.

You have to take the old advice to heart: you can't spend your time worrying about what others think. You only get one chance to go through life. Pray for guidance and let your conscience be your guide.

Spouse's Advice for the Family

Sharon

1. Every situation is different and every family needs to figure it out in their own way. We were blessed to have a close family that was willing to discuss the hard issues without accusing one another of doing something wrong. It's very important for the spouse or primary care giver to have support and to know that their support group is on the same team, not working against them.
2. Share your concerns with your immediate family. Don't keep everything inside yourself; that's very unhealthy. It's their right to know what is going on if you think your spouse has dementia, or any serious illness for that matter. You will need their help sooner or later.
3. Keep informed by reading everything you can, in books or on the internet. There is a mountain of information out

there if you look for it. It isn't always pleasant to read, but it still can be helpful. A person with diabetes becomes an expert on diabetes; a person living with a spouse with dementia can become an expert on dementia.

4. Talk to your family doctor if your spouse or parent shows signs of dementia. There might be other medical conditions causing forgetfulness and they need to be ruled out before a diagnosis can be made. When it comes to behavior changes, I found it very useful to write a summary of my observations and give that to the doctor before he actually saw my husband. It's very difficult to talk about negative behavior in front of the person. It also saved time and made the doctor visit more productive.

5. Develop a close relationship with a family doctor. We saw many specialists because there were other medical conditions present: severe arthritis resulting in bilateral knee replacements, heart issues requiring a pace maker, prostate cancer, in addition to the neurology issues. They were all necessary to rule out other problems, but I was relieved to have my family practice doctor put all the pieces in the puzzle.

6. Take advantage of the resources available. The respite care, the home health aides, and friends and neighbors were like a Godsend to me. Never refuse a friend or neighbor who volunteers to stay with your spouse so you can get away for a while.

7. Keep a journal. I started doing that to help me keep track of the different doctor visits, the different medications that were tried and just a time line to help my memory. I also found it very therapeutic to get everything down on paper. Sometimes I felt like I was going crazy but found it calming to write down my feelings.

8. Whatever your source of spiritual strength comes from, seek help from there. Prayer is a powerful source and truly, you never need to be alone in this journey.

Advice for a Person with Dementia

Mike – December 2010

You may not have dementia. You may have something else or you might just be aging naturally. However, there is a possibility you do have some form of dementia. Better to take it seriously than to ignore it and hope it goes away.

I have heard people say that dementia brought their family together. That may be true but I bet it was not a pleasant experience for the person with dementia. The disease progresses relentlessly. You will have good days and bad days. You may have long periods of time where it progresses slowly, a plateau. But you will not get better. You will not go back to the way you used to be.

A tremendous amount of money is being spent looking at ways to cure dementia. But most of it seems to be focused on slowing or preventing the spread of disease in the brain. That breakthrough will probably happen first. We are probably a lot farther away from a cure which reverses the disease.

You are not Stupid

The literature is full of really smart and successful people who have dementia. It almost seems dementia is more common in intense, introverted, smart people. Some ignorant people will treat you like you are stupid because of the disease. You will not be able to change their attitude any more than you can change their views on religion or politics.

You know what is going on way more than they think you do. You see things that others miss but have a hard time communicating them. You are frustrated because they have stopped listening to you. They assume everything you say is gibberish.

You are not the Boss Anymore

You may have been the leader of a huge company or a little church. Or you may have been queen of your own castle, the leader of your family who makes plans and determines the family's priorities. Whatever leadership role you had will be taken away from you by the disease.

You won't understand why things aren't being done "your way." It's not that your ideas are bad, in fact they might be very good. But you will increasingly feel like your ideas and suggestions are being ignored.

Your tendency will be to blame it on your family. They have already made up their minds that you are sick and now they are ganging up on you.

People will Talk about You

It will bug you to no end that people are talking about you behind your back. Then at some point they will talk about you in front of you, like you are not even there. You will feel like they are not even giving you a chance. Like they have acted as judge and jury and sentenced you to a death sentence of dementia with no chance for appeal.

Send You Away

Contrary to the way it seems, your family does not want to send you away. Partly because they still love and care for you, but also because sending you away will load them up with guilt. You have a common goal with your family: to keep you at home as long as possible.

Fight Authority

You may feel an urge to fight against your family. Adopt an "I'll show them" kind of an attitude. You may win a battle or two, but you will lose the war. Ultimately the disease will make it seem like the entire world is against you. You are better off trying to figure out how to work with the system instead of against it.

Passive and Pleasant

If your goal is to stay at home as long as possible, you will need to make yourself as easy to care for as possible. It may not be fair, but who said life is fair?

You will have to unlearn certain character traits, some of which may be deeply ingrained and contributed to your success in life. For example, assertiveness may have helped you to climb mountains in the business world. But it will not be appreciated by your family when you have dementia.

Another example might be your enjoyment of debating the issues of the day. You may have shared freely your opinion that democrats are bringing the country to ruin when you were healthy. The further along you get with the disease, the less people want to hear about it from you.

As much as it pains you, the more pleasant you are, the easier you are to care for, the longer you get to stay at home.

Family is on Your Side

Ultimately your family will seek assistance in caring for you. That may involve sending you to a long-term care facility. You will hate it. You will try to fight it. You will feel betrayed.

However, try to burn it into your mind that your family is on your side. They care deeply and love you intensely. It may not always seem like it, but they do. If they didn't, they would have sent you away a long time ago. Do what you can to make the disease as easy on them as possible and try not to take it out on them.

Grace and Dignity

Most people hope for a dignified end to their lives. Something which makes the world reflect back on what a good person they really were. I am not sure if dementia makes it easier or harder to live out your life with grace and dignity, but that is your challenge. Figure out how to make the most of it.

Or, as a beekeeper might say, "Some days the bees sting, and some days they make honey. You have to overlook the stings and appreciate the honey, because in the end, that's all we can do."

i. Eleanor Cooney – Death in Slow Motion, Eleanor Cooney 2003, Page 30
ii. Sue Miller – The Story of My Father, Sue Miller 2003. Page 19
iii. Sue Miller – The Story of My Father, Sue Miller 2003, Page 19
iv. www.longtermcarelink.net
v. Minneapolis Star Tribune – State faces unsustainable burden for long term care – December 14, 2010.
vi. Eleanor Cooney –Death in Slow Motion – Eleanor Cooney 2003. Page 175
vii. Eleanor Cooney – Death in Slow Motion, Eleanor Cooney 2003, Page 235
viii. Bible, Isaiah 40: 6

www.ingramcontent.com/pod-product-compliance
Lightning Source LLC
Chambersburg PA
CBHW060938040426
42445CB00011B/920